ENGLISH
FOR EVERYONE
JUNIOR
5 WORDS A DAY

FREE AUDIO
website and app

www.dk5words.com/us

ENGLISH
FOR EVERYONE
JUNIOR
5 WORDS A DAY

FREE AUDIO
website and app

www.dk5words.com/us

DK

For the curious

DK | Penguin
Random
House

Project Editor Elizabeth Blakemore
Editor Sophie Adam
Project Art Editor Anna Scully
Designer Annabel Schick
Illustrators Amy Child, Gus Scott
Managing Editor Christine Stroyan
Managing Art Editor Anna Hall
Production Editor Gillian Reid
Production Controller Sian Cheung
Senior Jacket Designer Suhita Dharamjit
Jacket Design Development Manager Sophia MTT
Publisher Andrew Macintyre
Art Director Karen Self
Publishing Director Jonathan Metcalf

First American Edition, 2021
Published in the United States by DK Publishing
1745 Broadway, 20th Floor, New York, NY 10019

Copyright © 2021 Dorling Kindersley Limited
DK, a Division of Penguin Random House LLC
23 24 18 17 16 15
015–318639–Mar/2021

A catalog record for this book is
available from the Library of Congress.
ISBN 978-0-7440-2754-9

DK books are available at special discounts
when purchased in bulk for sales promotions,
premiums, fund-raising, or educational use.
For details, contact: DK Publishing Special Markets,
1745 Broadway, 20th Floor, New York, NY 10019
SpecialSales@dk.com

Printed and bound in China

For the curious
www.dk.com

FSC
www.fsc.org
MIX
Paper | Supporting
responsible forestry
FSC™ C018179

This book was
made with Forest
Stewardship
Council™ certified
paper – one small
step in DK's
commitment to a
sustainable future.
For more
information go to
www.dk.com/
our-green-pledge

Contents

Max   Maria

How to use this book

English for Everyone Junior: 5 Words a Day is a vocabulary book for children that teaches and tests more than 1,000 English words. Words are taught in weekly units of 5 days.

Learning new vocabulary

On Days 1–4, the child will be presented with 20 new words, which are taught 5 words at a time through colorful illustrations.

1 First, listen to the words on the audio app or website, repeat the words out loud, and then write them out in the space below each word.

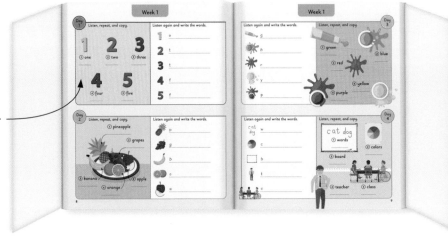

2 Next, use the book flaps to cover the illustrations and listen to the words again.

3 With the words still covered, try writing out each word from memory.

Testing new vocabulary

On Day 5, the child can practice the 20 new words
and reinforce their learning through fun exercises.

A variety of exercises are
used to test all 20 words.

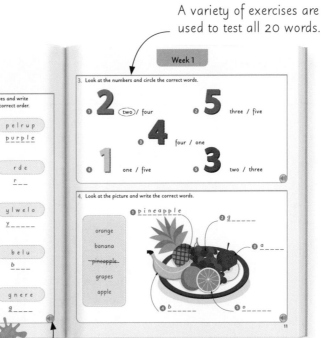

Once you have finished an exercise,
listen to the words again on the app
or website.

Answers to all the questions are
given at the back of the book.

Audio

Pronunciation is an important aspect of learning a new language. Audio for all the
words in this book is available on the **DK 5 Words** website and app. You should
encourage your child to listen to the audio and repeat the words out loud.

Access the audio recordings for free at **www.dk5words.com/us** or download the
DK 5 Words app from the App Store or Google Play.

FREE AUDIO
website and app

www.dk5words.com/us

Day 1

Listen, repeat, and copy.

1

① one
....

2

② two
....

3

③ three
....

4

④ four
....

5

⑤ five
....

Listen again and write the words.

1 o ....

2 t ....

3 t ....

4 f ....

5 f ....

Day 2

Listen, repeat, and copy.

① pineapple
....

② grapes
....

③ banana
....

④ orange
....

⑤ apple
....

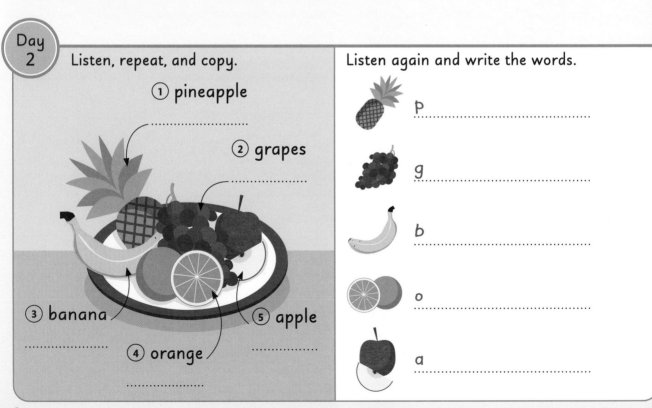

Listen again and write the words.

p ....

g ....

b ....

o ....

a ....

Listen again and write the words.

g ....

b ....

r ....

y ....

p ....

Listen, repeat, and copy.

① green

....

③ red

....

② blue

....

④ yellow

....

⑤ purple

....

Listen again and write the words.

cat dog   w ....

c ....

b ....

t ....

c ....

Listen, repeat, and copy.

cat dog
① words

....

② colors

....

③ board

....

④ teacher

....

⑤ class

....

Day 5

What can you remember from this week?

1. Look at the pictures and check the correct words.

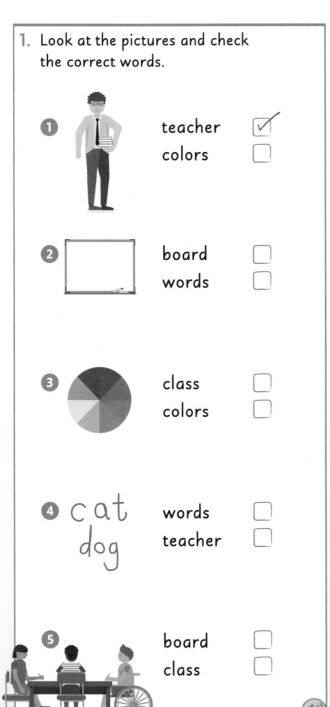

① teacher ☑
colors ☐

② board ☐
words ☐

③ class ☐
colors ☐

④ cat dog words ☐
teacher ☐

⑤ board ☐
class ☐

2. Look at the pictures and write the letters in the correct order.

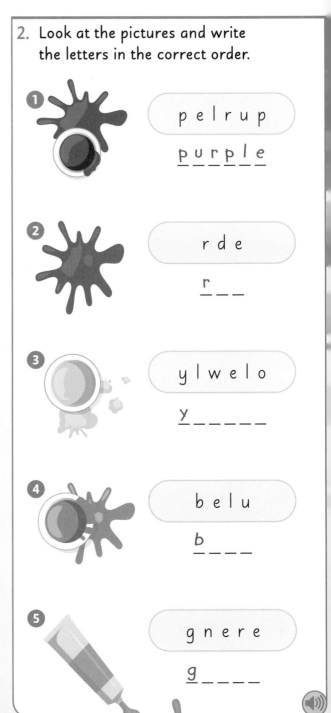

① p e l r u p
p u r p l e

② r d e
r _ _

③ y l w e l o
y _ _ _ _ _

④ b e l u
b _ _ _

⑤ g n e r e
g _ _ _ _

3. Look at the numbers and circle the correct words.

① **2** (two) / four

② **5** three / five

③ **4** four / one

④ **1** one / five

⑤ **3** two / three

4. Look at the picture and write the correct words.

① p i n e a p p l e

② g _ _ _ _ _ _

③ a _ _ _ _ _

④ b _ _ _ _ _ _

⑤ o _ _ _ _ _ _

orange

banana

~~pineapple~~

grapes

apple

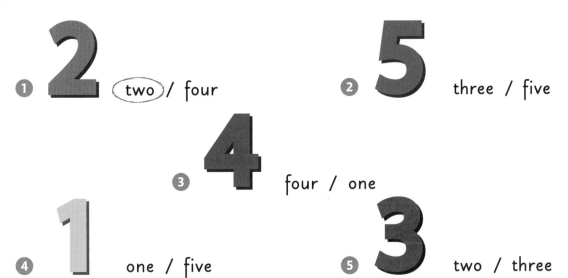

Day 1

Listen, repeat, and copy.

6 ① six
....

7 ② seven
....

8 ③ eight
....

9 ④ nine
....

10 ⑤ ten
....

Listen again and write the words.

6 s ....

7 s ....

8 e ....

9 n ....

10 t ....

Day 2

Listen, repeat, and copy.

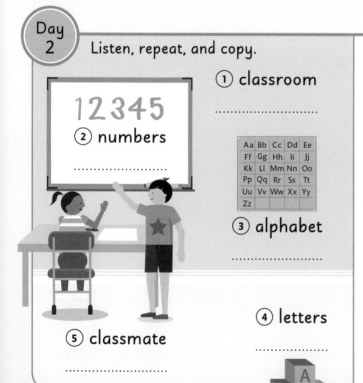

12345
② numbers
....

① classroom
....

③ alphabet
....

④ letters
....

⑤ classmate
....

Listen again and write the words.

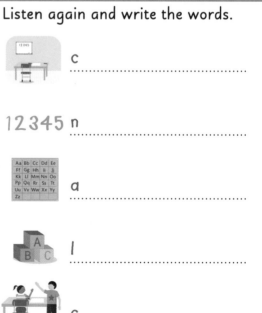

c ....

12345 n ....

a ....

l ....

c ....

Week 2

Listen again and write the words.

p ....

a ....

t ....

b ....

d ....

Listen, repeat, and copy.

① puppet
....

② action figure
....

③ teddy bear
....

④ board game
....

⑤ doll
....

Listen again and write the words.

p ....

p ....

p ....

c ....

p ....

Listen, repeat, and copy.

① pen
....

② paint
....

③ pencil
....

④ crayon
....

⑤ paper
....

Day 5

What can you remember from this week?

1. Look at the pictures and write the correct words.

| alphabet | ~~numbers~~ | classmate | letters | classroom |

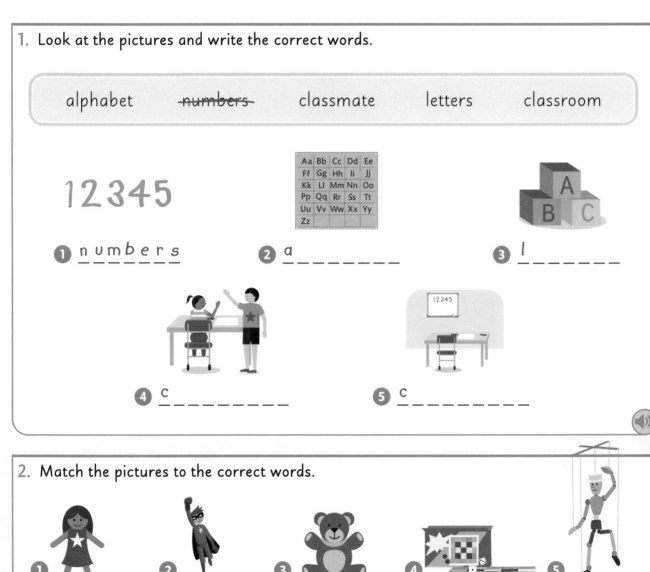

1 2 3 4 5

Aa	Bb	Cc	Dd	Ee
Ff	Gg	Hh	Ii	Jj
Kk	Ll	Mm	Nn	Oo
Pp	Qq	Rr	Ss	Tt
Uu	Vv	Ww	Xx	Yy
Zz				

1 n u m b e r s

2 a _ _ _ _ _ _ _ _

3 l _ _ _ _ _ _ _

4 c _ _ _ _ _ _ _ _ _

5 c _ _ _ _ _ _ _ _ _

2. Match the pictures to the correct words.

1   2   3   4   5

teddy bear   doll   action figure   puppet   board game

3. Read the words and check the correct pictures.

1 pen   A ☐   B ☑

2 crayon   A ☐   B ☐

3 paper   A ☐   B ☐

4 paint   A ☐   B ☐

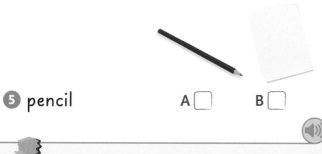

5 pencil   A ☐   B ☐

4. Look at the numbers and fill in the missing letters.

1  e i g h t

2  _ i _

3  n _ _ e

4  s _ v _ n

5  _ e _

15

Day 1

Listen, repeat, and copy.

① eleven ② twelve ③ thirteen

④ fourteen ⑤ fifteen

Listen again and write the words.

11   e

12   t

13   t

14   f

15   f

Day 2

Listen, repeat, and copy.

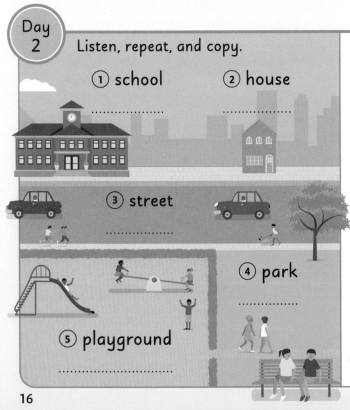

① school ② house

③ street

④ park

⑤ playground

Listen again and write the words.

s

h

s

p

p

Day 3

Listen again and write the words.

f ....

f ....

m ....

s ....

d ....

Listen, repeat, and copy.

① family

....

② father / dad   ③ mother / mom

④ son   ⑤ daughter

Day 4

Listen again and write the words.

d ....

c ....

s ....

c ....

w ....

Listen, repeat, and copy.

① draw   c a t   ② count

③ spell

④ color   ⑤ write

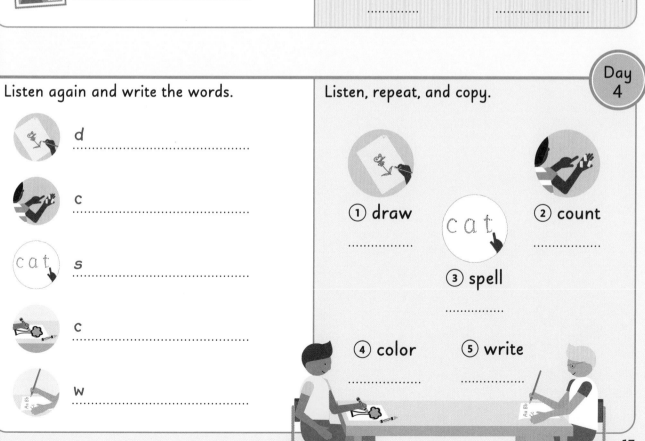

17

Day 5

What can you remember from this week?

1. Look at the pictures and check the correct words.

1. draw ✓
   spell ☐

2. color ☐
   count ☐

3. count ☐
   write ☐

4. color ☐
   spell ☐

5. draw ☐
   write ☐

2. Match the pictures to the correct words.

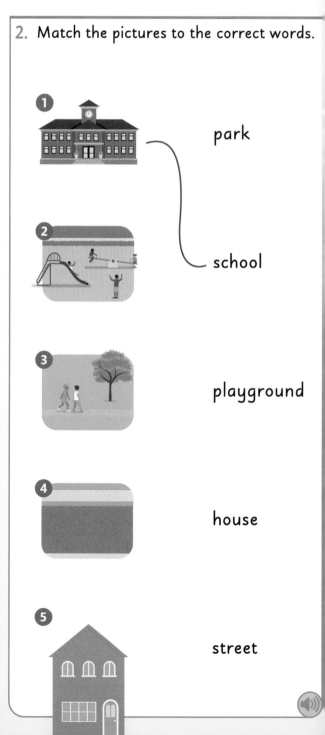

1 — school

2 park

3 playground

4 house

5 street

3. Look at the numbers and write the correct words.

11

① e l e v e n

13

② t _ _ _ _ _ _ _ _

15

③ f _ _ _ _ _ _

14

④ f _ _ _ _ _ _ _ _

12

⑤ t _ _ _ _ _ _

4. Look at the pictures and write the correct words.

① f a m i l y

son

~~family~~

father

daughter

mother

② f _ _ _ _ _ _

③ m _ _ _ _ _ _

④ s _ _ _

⑤ d _ _ _ _ _ _ _ _

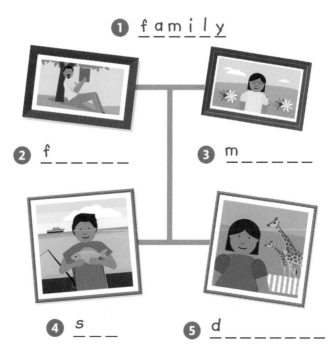

Day 1

Listen, repeat, and copy.

16
① sixteen
....

17
② seventeen
....

18
③ eighteen
....

19
④ nineteen
....

20
⑤ twenty
....

Listen again and write the words.

16 s ....

17 s ....

18 e ....

19 n ....

20 t ....

Day 2

Listen, repeat, and copy.

① cow
....

② goat
....

③ sheep
....

④ chicken
....

⑤ horse
....

Listen again and write the words.

 c ....

 g ....

 s ....

 c ....

 h ....

Listen again and write the words.

b ....

b ....

l ....

d ....

k ....

Listen, repeat, and copy.

① bedroom

....

② bathroom

....

③ living room

....

④ dining room

....

⑤ kitchen

....

Listen again and write the words.

b ....

w ....

b ....

p ....

o ....

Listen, repeat, and copy.

① black

....

② white

....

③ brown

....

④ pink

....

⑤ orange

....

Day 5

What can you remember from this week?

---

1. Look at the pictures and fill in the missing letters.

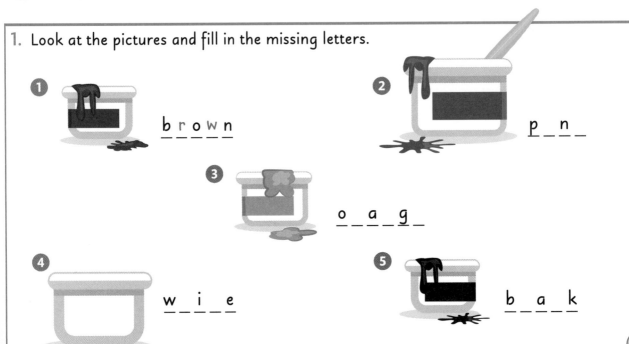

① b r o w n

② p _ n _

③ o _ a _ g _

④ w _ i _ e

⑤ b _ a _ k

---

2. Read the words and check the correct pictures.

❶ **bedroom**

A ☐   B ☑

❷ **kitchen**

A ☐   B ☐

❸ **bathroom**

A ☐   B ☐

❹ **living room**

A ☐   B ☐

❺ **dining room**

A ☐   B ☐

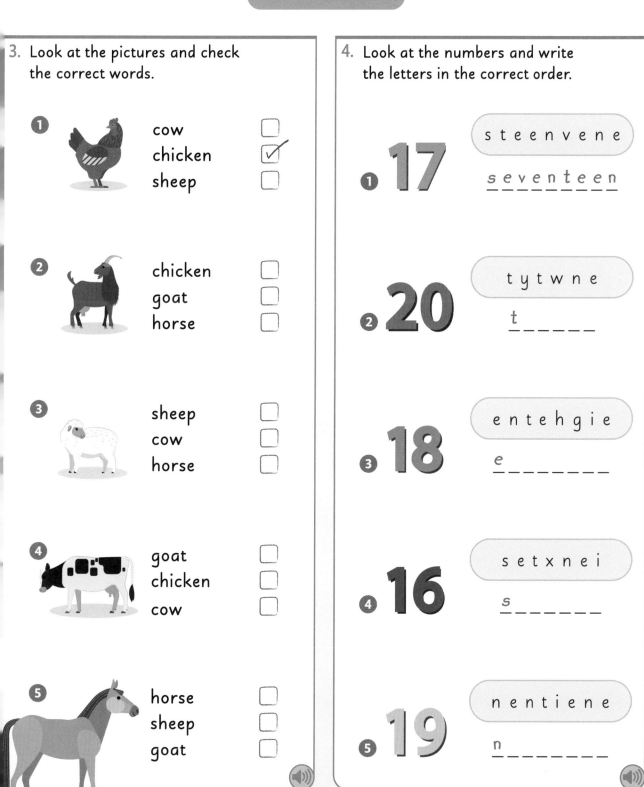

3. Look at the pictures and check the correct words.

1. cow ☐
   chicken ☑
   sheep ☐

2. chicken ☐
   goat ☐
   horse ☐

3. sheep ☐
   cow ☐
   horse ☐

4. goat ☐
   chicken ☐
   cow ☐

5. horse ☐
   sheep ☐
   goat ☐

4. Look at the numbers and write the letters in the correct order.

1. 17 steenvene
   s e v e n t e e n

2. 20 tytwne
   t _ _ _ _ _ _

3. 18 entehgie
   e _ _ _ _ _ _ _

4. 16 setxnei
   s _ _ _ _ _ _

5. 19 nentiene
   n _ _ _ _ _ _ _

Day 1

Listen, repeat, and copy.

① zebra

② giraffe

③ lion

④ hippo

⑤ elephant

Listen again and write the words.

z ....

g ....

l ....

h ....

e ....

Day 2

Listen, repeat, and copy.

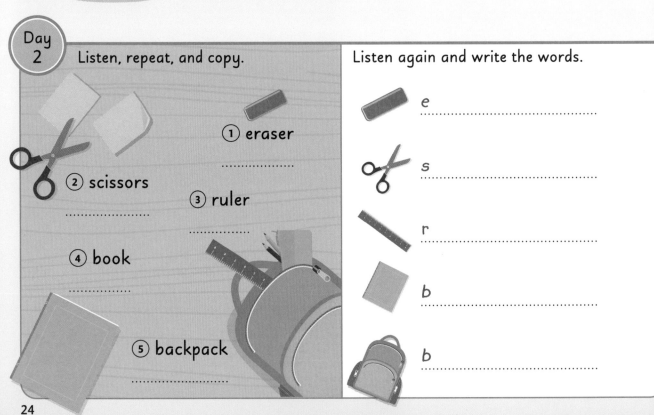

① eraser

② scissors

③ ruler

④ book

⑤ backpack

Listen again and write the words.

e ....

s ....

r ....

b ....

b ....

Listen again and write the words.

 a ....

 l ....

 l ....

 t ....

 p ....

Listen, repeat, and copy.

 ① answer

 ② listen

....

 ③ learn

 ④ teach

....

⑤ point

....

Listen again and write the words.

 m ....

 p ....

 k ....

 w ....

 c ....

Listen, repeat, and copy.

① mango ② pear ③ kiwi

....

④ watermelon ⑤ coconut

....

Day 5

What can you remember from this week?

1. Match the pictures to the correct words.

 ①   lion

 ②   zebra

 ③   elephant

 ④   hippo

 ⑤   giraffe

2. Look at the pictures and write the correct words.

 ①   s _ _ _ _ _ _ _

 ②   b _ _ _ _

 ③   r _ _ _ _

 ④   e _ _ _ _ _

 ⑤   b _ _ _ _ _ _ _

3. Look at the pictures and write the correct words.

answer	listen	point	teach	learn

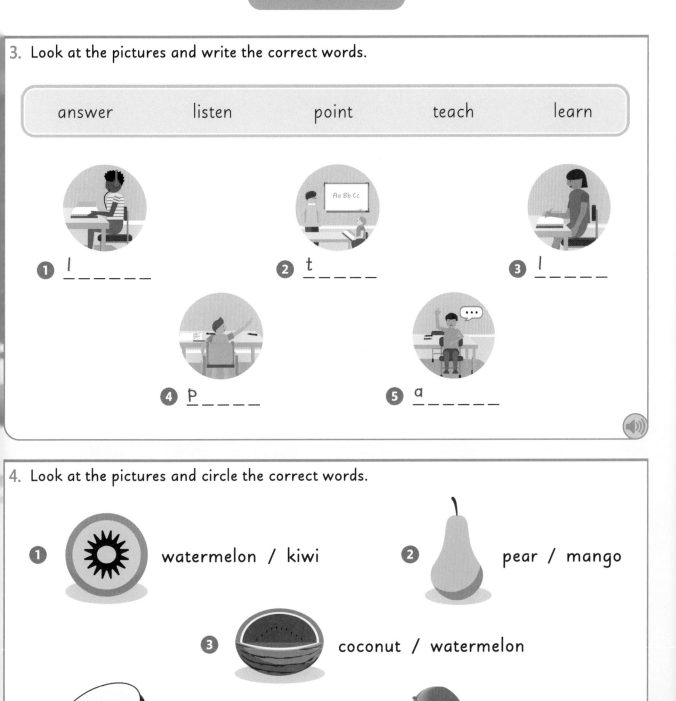

① l _ _ _ _ _ _

② t _ _ _ _ _

③ l _ _ _ _ _

④ P _ _ _ _ _

⑤ a _ _ _ _ _ _

4. Look at the pictures and circle the correct words.

① watermelon / kiwi

② pear / mango

③ coconut / watermelon

④ coconut / pear

⑤ kiwi / mango

Week 6

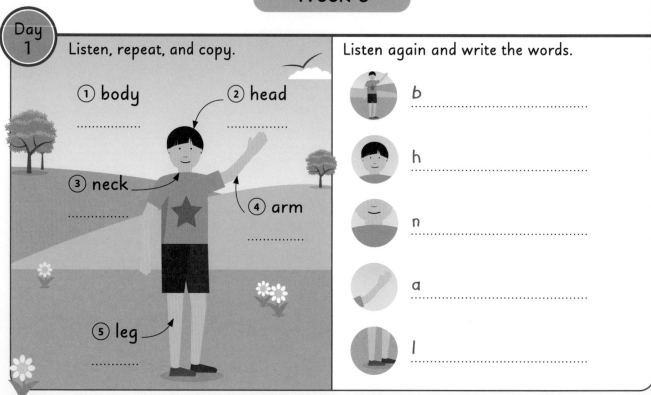

Day 1

Listen, repeat, and copy.

① body

② head

③ neck

④ arm

⑤ leg

Listen again and write the words.

b _____

h _____

n _____

a _____

l _____

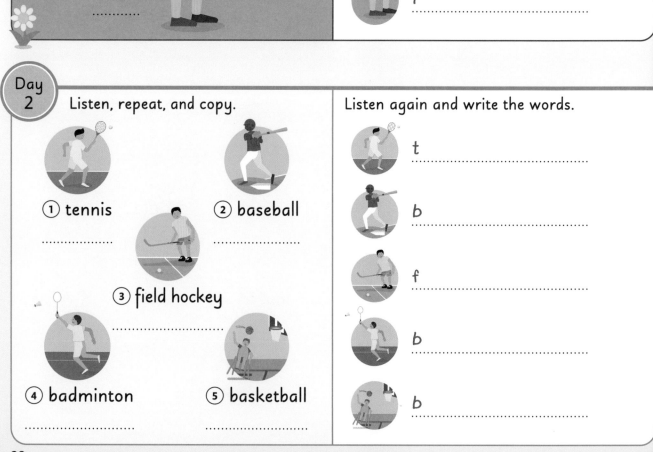

Day 2

Listen, repeat, and copy.

① tennis

② baseball

③ field hockey

④ badminton

⑤ basketball

Listen again and write the words.

t _____

b _____

f _____

b _____

b _____

Week 6

Listen again and write the words.

s ....

k ....

s ....

s ....

b ....

Listen, repeat, and copy.

① seagull
....

② kite
....

③ ship
....

④ sea
....

⑤ ball
....

Listen again and write the words.

d ....

c ....

g ....

r ....

p ....

Listen, repeat, and copy.

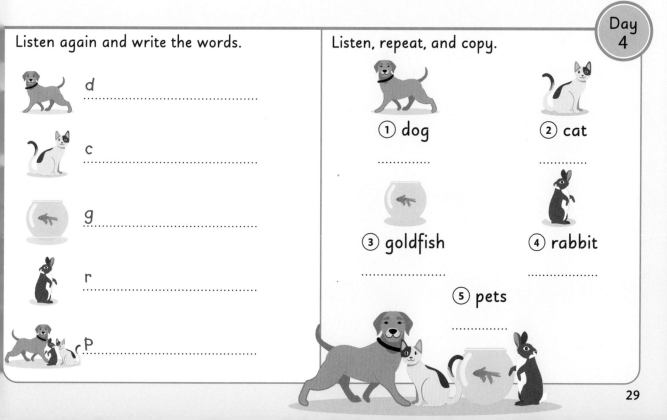

① dog
....

② cat
....

③ goldfish
....

④ rabbit
....

⑤ pets
....

29

Week 6

What can you remember from this week?

---

1. Read the words and check the correct pictures.

1 cat

A ☐   B ☐

2 rabbit

A ☐   B ☐

3 dog

A ☐   B ☐

4 pets

A ☐   B ☐

5 goldfish

A ☐   B ☐

---

2. Look at the pictures and fill in the missing letters.

1    h _ _ a _

2    _ e _

3   b _ d _

4    _ r _

5    n _ c _

3. Look at the pictures and check the correct words.

1.
baseball ☐
field hockey ☐

2.
tennis ☐
badminton ☐

3.
basketball ☐
baseball ☐

4.
tennis ☐
basketball ☐

5.
badminton ☐
field hockey ☐

4. Look at the pictures and write the correct words.

1.
s _ _ _

2.
s _ _ _ _ _ _

3.
k _ _ _ _

4.
s _ _ _ _

5.
b _ _ _ _

31

Day 1

Listen, repeat, and copy.

① clothes

....

② socks

③ pajamas

....

④ jeans   ⑤ underwear

....

Listen again and write the words.

c ....

s ....

p ....

j ....

u ....

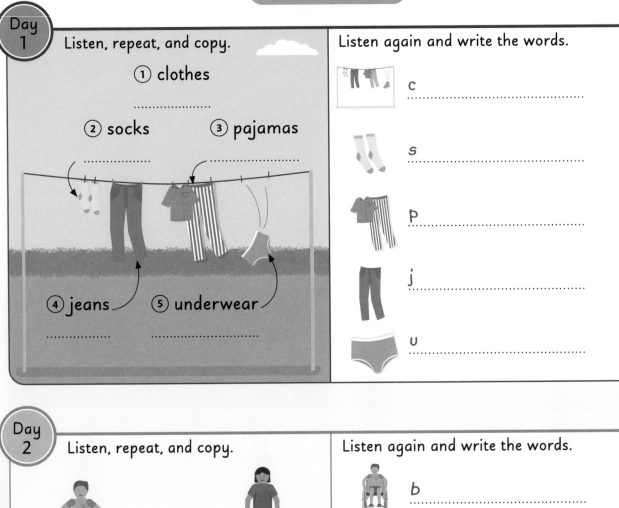

Day 2

Listen, repeat, and copy.

① boy   ② girl

....

③ baby

....

④ man   ⑤ woman

....

Listen again and write the words.

b ....

g ....

b ....

m ....

w ....

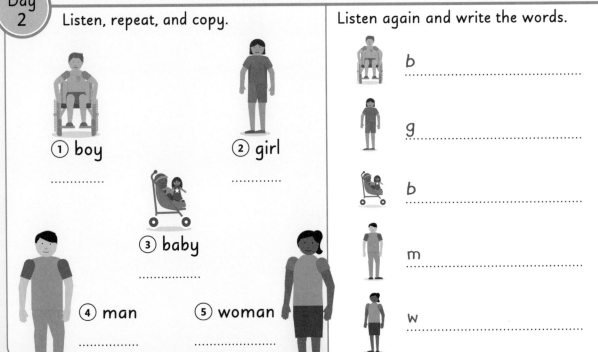

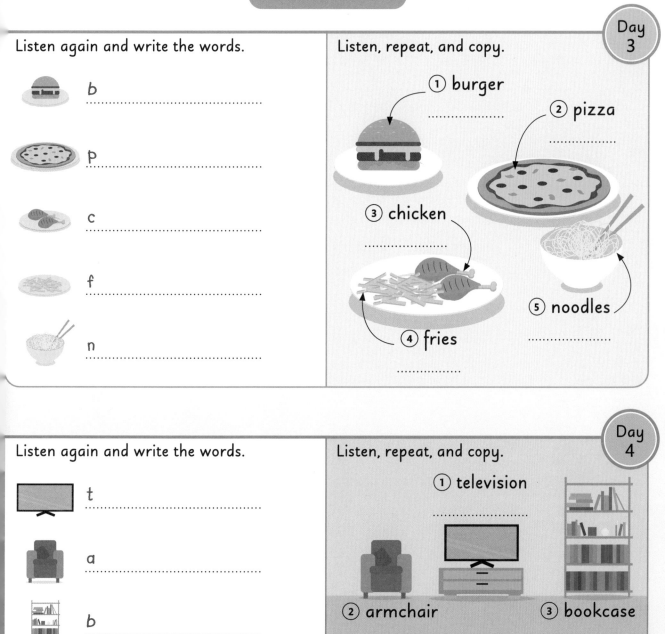

Week 7

Listen again and write the words.

b ....

p ....

c ....

f ....

n ....

Listen, repeat, and copy.

① burger ....

② pizza ....

③ chicken ....

④ fries ....

⑤ noodles ....

Listen again and write the words.

t ....

a ....

b ....

r ....

c ....

Listen, repeat, and copy.

① television ....

② armchair ....

③ bookcase ....

④ rug ....

⑤ couch ....

Day 5

What can you remember from this week?

1. Look at the pictures and fill in the missing letters.

❶    g _ r _

❷    _ a _

❸    _ o _

❹   b _ b _

❺    w _ m _ n

2. Read the words and check the correct pictures.

❶ jeans   A ☐   B ☐

❷ underwear   A ☐   B ☐

❸ pajamas   A ☐   B ☐

❹ socks   A ☐   B ☐

❺ clothes   A ☐   B ☐

3. Look at the pictures and write the correct words.

| rug | couch | television | bookcase | armchair |

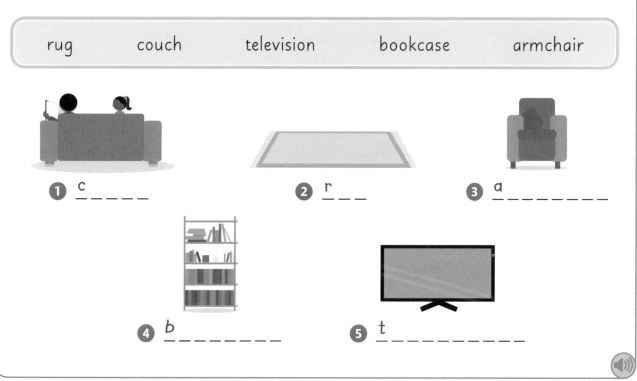

1 c _ _ _ _ _

2 r _ _ _

3 a _ _ _ _ _ _ _ _

4 b _ _ _ _ _ _ _

5 t _ _ _ _ _ _ _ _ _

4. Look at the pictures and circle the correct words.

1  burger / pizza

2  pizza / noodles

3 burger / fries

4  fries / chicken

5  noodles / chicken

Day 1

Listen, repeat, and copy.

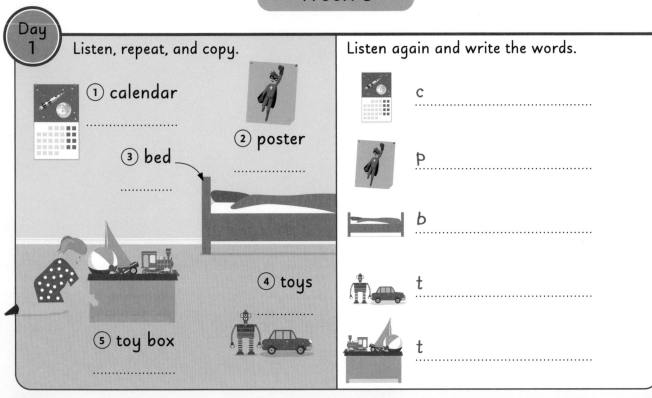

① calendar

② poster

③ bed

④ toys

⑤ toy box

Listen again and write the words.

c ....

p ....

b ....

t ....

t ....

Day 2

Listen, repeat, and copy.

① day

② night

③ morning

④ afternoon

⑤ evening

Listen again and write the words.

d ....

n ....

m ....

a ....

e ....

Listen again and write the words.

o ....

c ....

p ....

s ....

s ....

Listen, repeat, and copy.

① open

② close

③ pick up

④ sit down

⑤ stand up

Listen again and write the words.

j ....

m ....

t ....

b ....

f ....

Listen, repeat, and copy.

① jungle

② monkey

③ tiger

④ bear

⑤ frog

Day 5

What can you remember from this week?

1. Look at the pictures and write the correct words.

① t _ _ _ _ _

② f _ _ _ _

③ m _ _ _ _ _ _

④ j _ _ _ _ _ _

⑤ b _ _ _ _

2. Read the words and check the correct pictures.

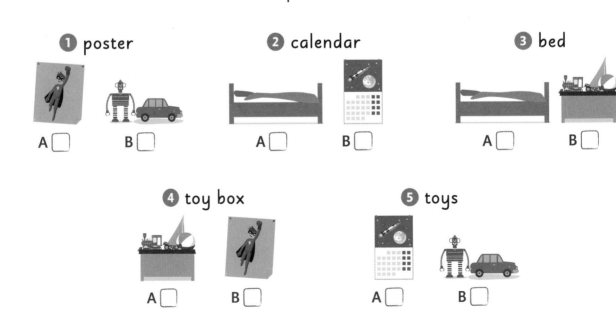

① poster

A ☐   B ☐

② calendar

A ☐   B ☐

③ bed

A ☐   B ☐

④ toy box

A ☐   B ☐

⑤ toys

A ☐   B ☐

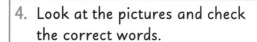

3. Look at the pictures and fill in the missing letters.

s _ t _ _ o _ n

o _ e _

c _ o _ e

p _ c _ u _

s _ a _ d _ _ p

4. Look at the pictures and check the correct words.

afternoon
evening □

night □
afternoon

night □
morning □

day
evening □

morning □
day

Week 9

Day 1

Listen, repeat, and copy.

① T-shirt

....

② dress

....

③ shorts

....

④ sandals

....

⑤ shoes

....

Listen again and write the words.

T- ....

d ....

s ....

s ....

s ....

Day 2

Listen, repeat, and copy.

① kick

....

② bounce

....

③ catch

....

④ throw

....

⑤ hit

....

Listen again and write the words.

k ....

b ....

c ....

t ....

h ....

Listen again and write the words.

g...

g...

g...

g...

g...

Listen, repeat, and copy.

① grandparents

....

② grandmother   ③ grandfather

④ grandson   ⑤ granddaughter

Listen again and write the words.

p...

y...

o...

n...

s...

Listen, repeat, and copy.

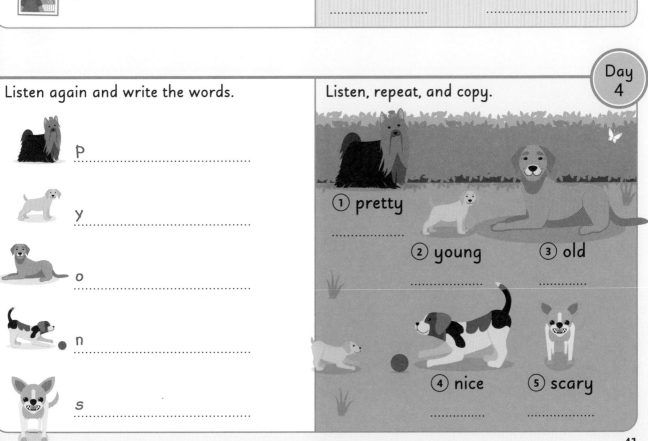

① pretty

② young   ③ old

④ nice   ⑤ scary

Day 5

What can you remember from this week?

1. Look at the pictures and write the correct words.

❶ g _ _ _ _ _ _ _ _ _ _ _ _

grandparents

grandson

grandfather

granddaughter

grandmother

❷ g _ _ _ _ _ _ _ _ _ _ _

❸ g _ _ _ _ _ _ _ _ _ _ _

❹ g _ _ _ _ _ _ _ _

❺ g _ _ _ _ _ _ _ _ _ _ _

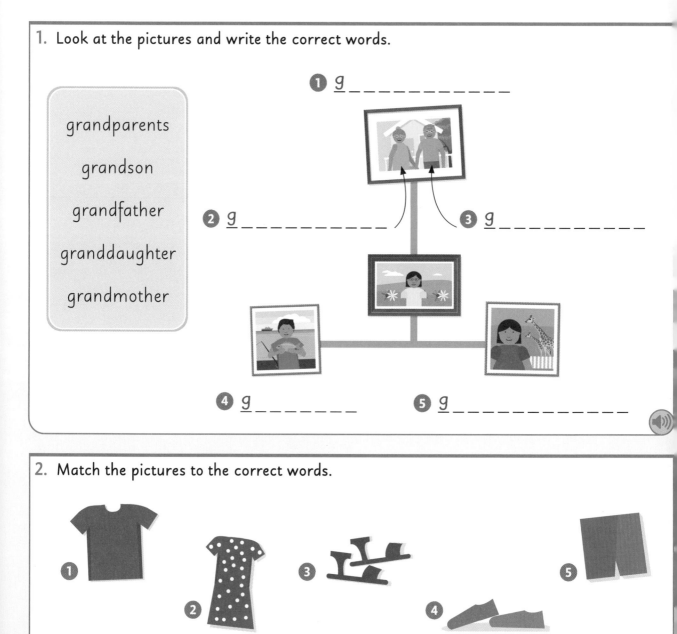

2. Match the pictures to the correct words.

❶

❷

❸

❹

❺

sandals   T-shirt   shorts   dress   shoes

3. Look at the pictures and check the correct words.

① pretty ☐
old ☐

② scary ☐
old ☐

③ scary ☐
nice ☐

④ pretty ☐
young ☐

⑤ nice ☐
young ☐

4. Look at the pictures and write the correct words.

kick   catch   hit
    throw   bounce

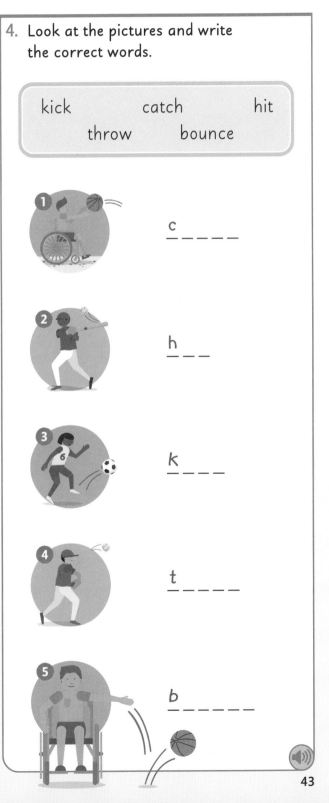

① c _ _ _ _ _

② h _ _

③ k _ _ _

④ t _ _ _ _ _

⑤ b _ _ _ _ _ _

43

Week 10

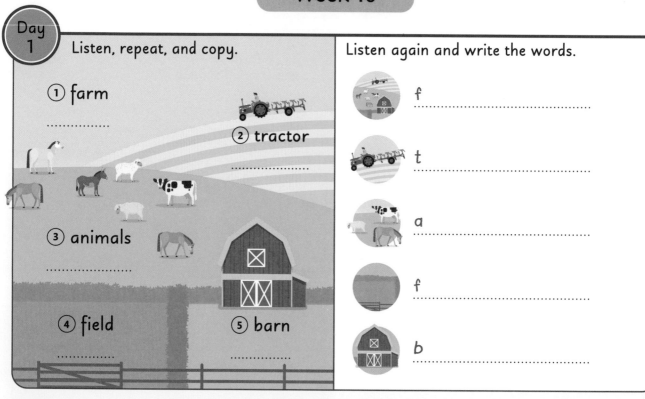

Day 1

Listen, repeat, and copy.

① farm

② tractor

③ animals

④ field

⑤ barn

Listen again and write the words.

f ....

t ....

a ....

f ....

b ....

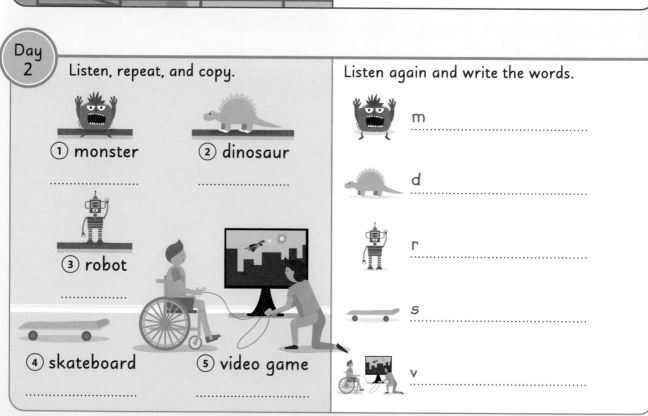

Day 2

Listen, repeat, and copy.

① monster

② dinosaur

③ robot

④ skateboard

⑤ video game

Listen again and write the words.

m ....

d ....

r ....

s ....

v ....

44

Week 10

Day 3

Listen again and write the words.

c ....

c ....

c ....

a ....

m ....

Listen, repeat, and copy.

① cross
....

② circle
....

③ check
....

④ add
....

⑤ match
....

Day 4

Listen again and write the words.

m ....

p ....

w ....

c ....

p ....

Listen, repeat, and copy.

① men
....

② people
....

③ women
....

④ children
....

⑤ person
....

45

Day 5

What can you remember from this week?

1. Look at the pictures and write the letters in the correct order.

① p n s o r e

p _ _ _ _ _ _

② w n e m o

w _ _ _ _ _

③ c r e h n i l d

c _ _ _ _ _ _ _ _

④ p e l o p e

p _ _ _ _ _ _

⑤ m n e

m _ _ _

2. Read the words and check the correct pictures.

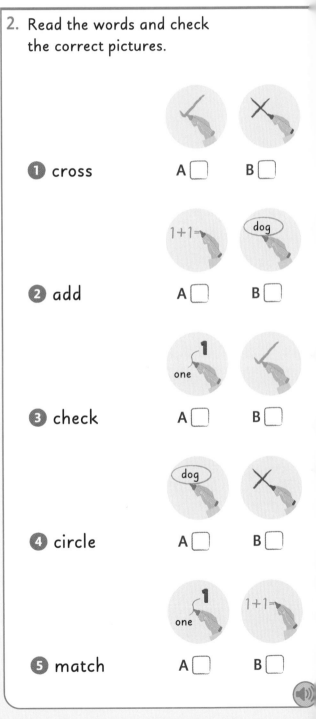

① cross   A ☐   B ☐

② add   A ☐   B ☐

③ check   A ☐   B ☐

④ circle   A ☐   B ☐

⑤ match   A ☐   B ☐

3. Look at the pictures and fill in the missing letters.

 t _ a _ t _ r

 f _ e _ d

 f _ r _

 a _ i _ a _ s

 b _ r _

4. Look at the pictures and circle the correct words.

 dinosaur
robot

 skateboard
dinosaur

 monster
video game

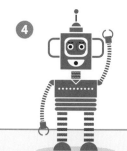 robot
video game

 monster
skateboard

Day 1

Listen, repeat, and copy.

① sing

② dance

③ play the piano

④ play the guitar

⑤ take a photo

Listen again and write the words.

s ....

d ....

p ....

p ....

t ....

Day 2

Listen, repeat, and copy.

① clean

② dirty

③ beautiful

④ big

⑤ small

Listen again and write the words.

c ....

d ....

b ....

b ....

s ....

Listen again and write the words.

e ....

e ....

f ....

l ....

n ....

Listen, repeat, and copy.

① eye

② ear

③ face

④ lips

⑤ nose

Listen again and write the words.

s ....

s ....

p ....

b ....

j ....

Listen, repeat, and copy.

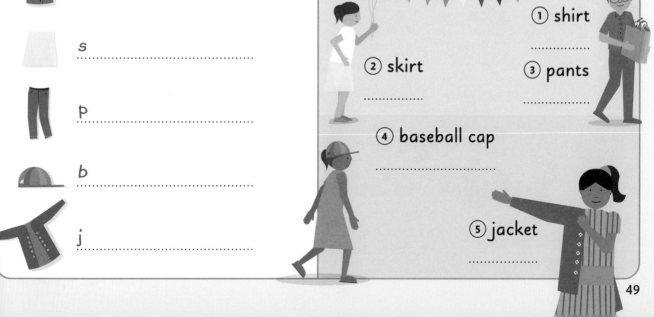

① shirt

② skirt

③ pants

④ baseball cap

⑤ jacket

Week 11

Day 5

What can you remember from this week?

1. Look at the pictures and write the correct words.

1 e _ _ _

2 l _ _ _ _

3 n _ _ _ _

4 e _ _ _

5 f _ _ _ _

2. Read the words and check the correct pictures.

1 sing

A ☐   B ☐

2 play the piano

A ☐   B ☐

3 dance

A ☐   B ☐

4 play the guitar

A ☐   B ☐

5 take a photo

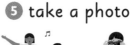

A ☐   B ☐

50

3. Look at the pictures and write the letters in the correct order.

 ① b f u t i u l a e

b _ _ _ _ _ _ _ _ _

 ② c e n l a

c _ _ _ _ _

 ③ s l a m l

s _ _ _ _ _

 ④ d t i y r

d _ _ _ _ _

 ⑤ b g i

b _ _ _

4. Match the pictures to the correct words.

 ①   skirt

 ②   shirt

 ③   baseball cap

 ④   jacket

 ⑤   pants

Week 12

Day 1

Listen, repeat, and copy.

① breakfast

② egg

③ cereal

④ sausage

⑤ pancake

Listen again and write the words.

b ....

e ....

c ....

s ....

p ....

Day 2

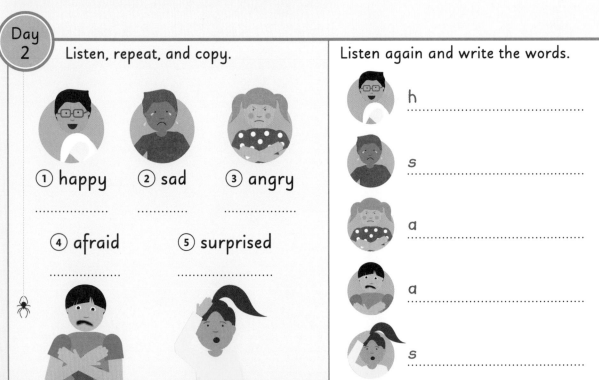

Listen, repeat, and copy.

① happy   ② sad   ③ angry

④ afraid   ⑤ surprised

Listen again and write the words.

h ....

s ....

a ....

a ....

s ....

Listen again and write the words.

i ....

n ....

b ....

i ....

o ....

Listen, repeat, and copy.

① in
....

② next to
....

③ behind
....

④ in front of
....

⑤ on
....

Listen again and write the words.

a ....

b ....

e ....

a ....

g ....

Listen, repeat, and copy.

① apartment building
....

② balcony
....

③ elevator
....

④ apartment
....

⑤ ground floor
....

Day 5

What can you remember from this week?

1. Look at the pictures and write the correct words.

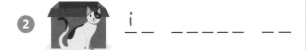

in   behind   on
in front of   next to

①  i _ _

② i _ _ _ _ _ _ _ _ _ _

③ b _ _ _ _ _ _

④  n _ _ _ _ _ _

⑤  o _ _

2. Look at the pictures and check the correct words.

①  cereal ☐
egg ☐

② 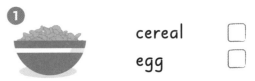 pancake ☐
breakfast ☐

③  egg ☐
sausage ☐

④  pancake ☐
cereal ☐

⑤  breakfast ☐
sausage ☐

Week 12

3. Look at the pictures and circle the correct words.

 1. balcony / apartment building

 2. apartment / elevator

 3. apartment building / ground floor

 4. ground floor / elevator

 5. balcony / apartment

4. Look at the pictures and fill in the missing letters.

1. s _ r _ r _ s _ d

2. s _ _ d

3. a _ r _ i _

4. h _ _ p _ _ y

5. a _ _ g _ _ y

55

Day 1

Listen, repeat, and copy.

① lunch

....

② sandwich

....

③ snack

....

④ yogurt

....

⑤ fruit

....

Listen again and write the words.

l ....

s ....

s ....

y ....

f ....

Day 2

Listen, repeat, and copy.

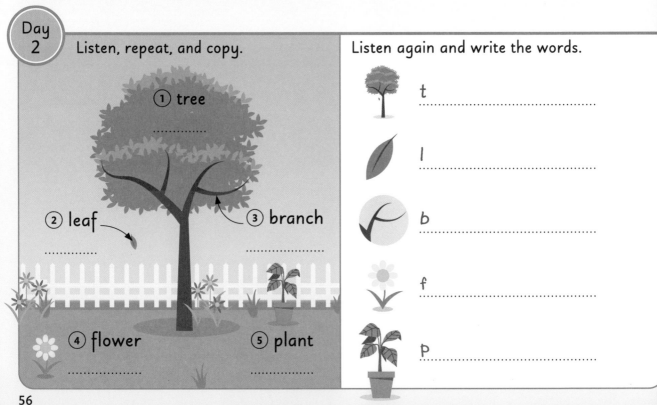

① tree

....

② leaf

....

③ branch

....

④ flower

....

⑤ plant

....

Listen again and write the words.

t ....

l ....

b ....

f ....

p ....

Day 3

Listen again and write the words.

d ....

c ....

w ....

r ....

c ....

Listen, repeat, and copy.

① drive

....

② catch a bus

....

③ walk

....

④ run

....

⑤ cycle

....

Day 4

Listen again and write the words.

r ....

s ....

w ....

f ....

r ....

Listen, repeat, and copy.

① rain

....

② storm

....

③ wind

....

④ fog

....

⑤ rainbow

....

Day 5

What can you remember from this week?

1. Read the words and check the correct pictures.

❶ drive

A ☐   B ☐

❷ walk

A ☐   B ☐

❸ run

A ☐   B ☐

❹ catch a bus

A ☐   B ☐

❺ cycle

A ☐   B ☐

2. Look at the pictures and write the correct words.

❶ l

❷ b

❸ t ____

❹ p

❺ f

3. Look at the pictures and write the correct words.

rain	storm	wind
	rainbow	fog

1 s _ _ _ _ _

2 w _ _ _

3 f _ _

4 r _ _ _ _

5 r _ _ _ _ _ _

4. Match the pictures to the correct words.

1  fruit

2  snack

3  lunch

4  yogurt

5  sandwich

Day 1

Listen, repeat, and copy.

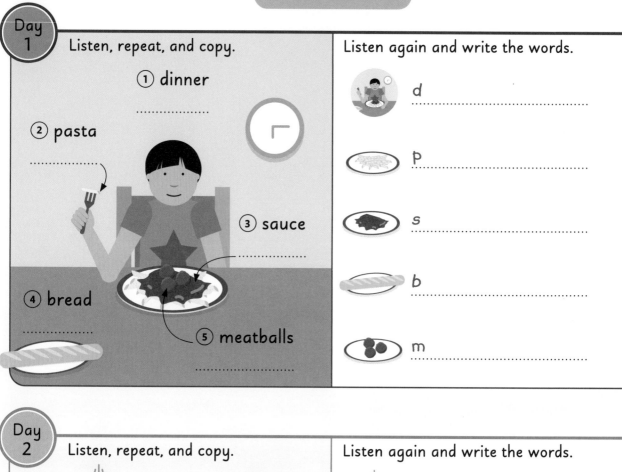

① dinner

② pasta

③ sauce

④ bread

⑤ meatballs

Listen again and write the words.

d ....

p ....

s ....

b ....

m ....

Day 2

Listen, repeat, and copy.

① painting

② drawing

③ sports

④ dancing

⑤ hobbies

Listen again and write the words.

p ....

d ....

s ....

d ....

h ....

Week 14

Listen again and write the words.

u ....

a ....

c ....

b ....

s ....

Listen, repeat, and copy.

① uncle   ② aunt

....

③ cousin

....

④ brother   ⑤ sister

....

Listen again and write the words.

r ....

s ....

h ....

y ....

f ....

Listen, repeat, and copy.

① roof

....

② shed

....

③ home

....

④ yard

....

⑤ fence

....

Day 5 What can you remember from this week?

1. Look at the pictures and circle the correct words.

roof / yard

shed / fence

yard / home

roof / shed

home / fence

2. Look at the pictures and write the letters in the correct order.

d g n r w a i

d _ _ _ _ _ _

d n g i c n a

d _ _ _ _ _ _

p t i a n g i n

p _ _ _ _ _ _ _

s t o r p s

s _ _ _ _ _

h s b i e o b

h _ _ _ _ _ _

3. Look at the pictures and write the correct words.

aunt

brother

cousin

uncle

sister

1 u _ _ _ _ _ _

2 a _ _ _ _

3 c _ _ _ _ _ _ _

4 b _ _ _ _ _ _ _ _

5 s _ _ _ _ _ _

4. Match the pictures to the correct words.

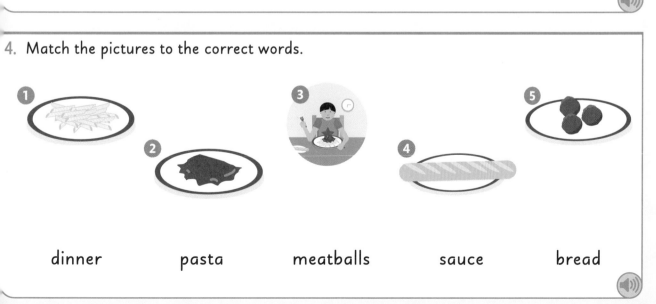

dinner   pasta   meatballs   sauce   bread

Week 15

Day 1

Listen, repeat, and copy.

Listen again and write the words.

① play

② climb

③ run

④ jump

⑤ skip

p ....

c ....

r ....

j ....

s ....

Day 2

Listen, repeat, and copy.

Listen again and write the words.

① sneakers

② tennis racket

③ bat

④ helmet

⑤ roller skates

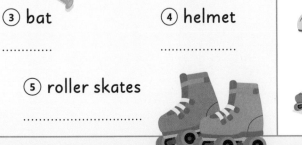

s ....

t ....

b ....

h ....

r ....

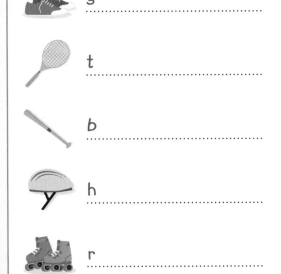

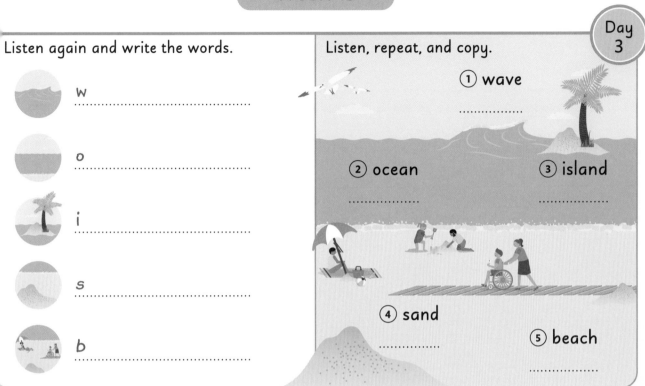

Day 3

Listen again and write the words.

w
....

o
....

i
....

s
....

b
....

Listen, repeat, and copy.

① wave
....

② ocean
....

③ island
....

④ sand
....

⑤ beach
....

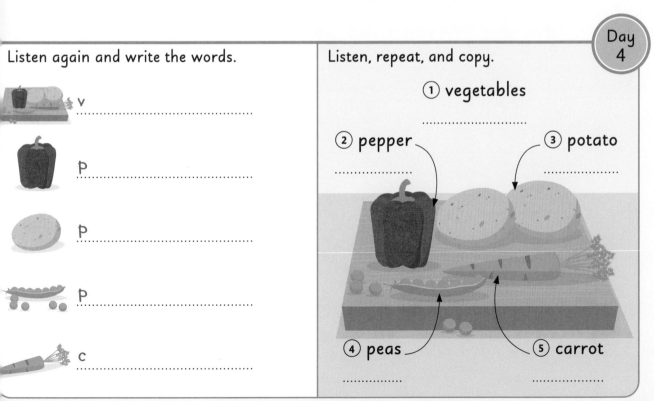

Day 4

Listen again and write the words.

v
....

p
....

p
....

p
....

c
....

Listen, repeat, and copy.

① vegetables
....

② pepper
....

③ potato
....

④ peas
....

⑤ carrot
....

Day 5

What can you remember from this week?

1. Look at the pictures and check the correct words.

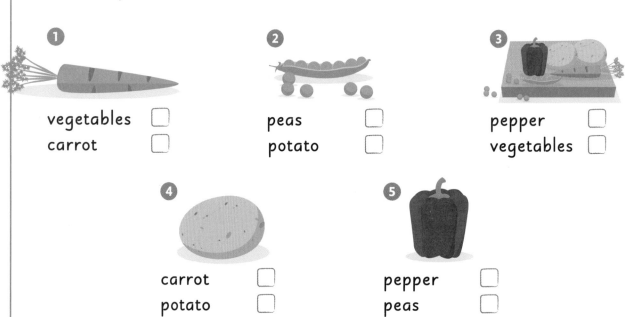

① vegetables ☐
carrot ☐

② peas ☐
potato ☐

③ pepper ☐
vegetables ☐

④ carrot ☐
potato ☐

⑤ pepper ☐
peas ☐

2. Look at the pictures and fill in the missing letters.

① o _ e _ n

② w _ _ v _

③ b _ a _ h

④ s _ n _

⑤ i _ l _ n _

3. Match the pictures to the correct words.

 1 bat

 2 helmet

 3 sneakers

 4 roller skates

 5 tennis racket

4. Look at the pictures and write the correct words.

 1 r _ _

 2 s _ _ _

 3 p _ _ _

 4 c _ _ _ _

 5 j _ _ _

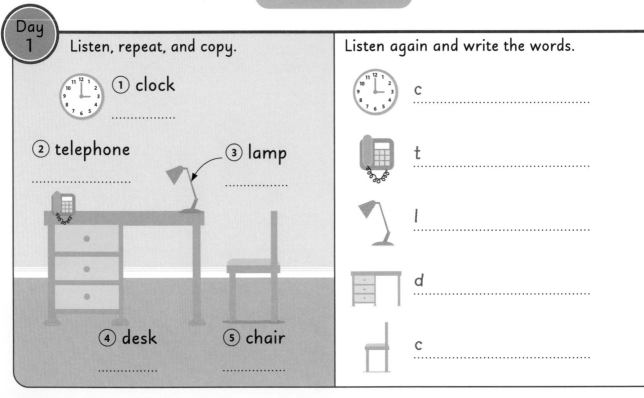

Day 1

Listen, repeat, and copy.

① clock

② telephone

③ lamp

④ desk

⑤ chair

Listen again and write the words.

c ....

t ....

l ....

d ....

c ....

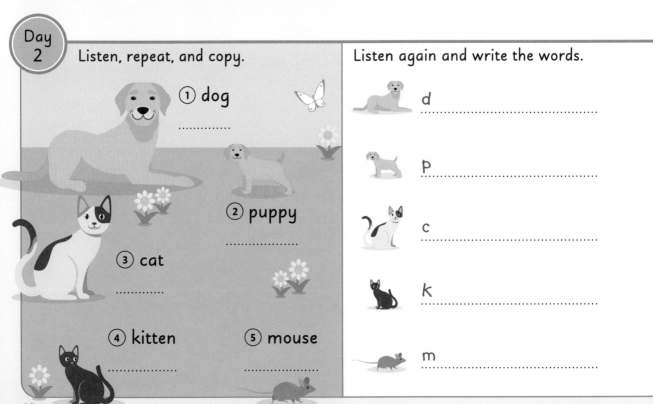

Day 2

Listen, repeat, and copy.

① dog

② puppy

③ cat

④ kitten

⑤ mouse

Listen again and write the words.

d ....

p ....

c ....

k ....

m ....

Listen again and write the words.

w ....

d ....

c ....

e ....

d ....

Listen, repeat, and copy.

① wash ....

② dry ....

③ cook ....

④ eat ....

⑤ drink ....

Listen again and write the words.

p ....

b ....

g ....

c ....

i ....

Listen, repeat, and copy.

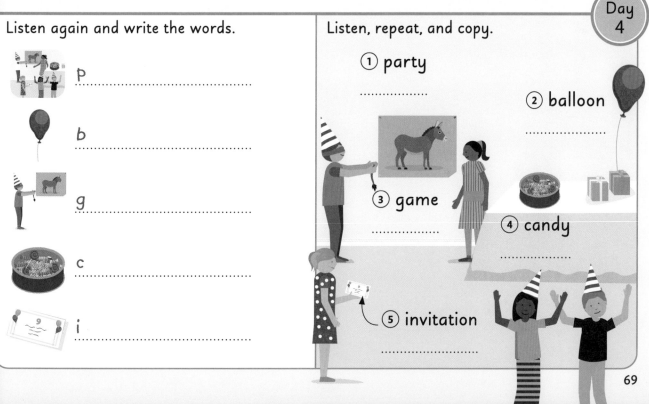

① party ....

② balloon ....

③ game ....

④ candy ....

⑤ invitation ....

Day 5

What can you remember from this week?

1. Look at the pictures and check the correct words.

1. candy ☐
   game ☐

2. balloon ☐
   party ☐

3. party ☐
   game ☐

4. invitation ☐
   candy ☐

5. invitation ☐
   balloon ☐

2. Look at the pictures and write the letters in the correct order.

1. c k o o
   c _ _ _ _

2. e t a
   e _ _ _

3. w h s a
   w _ _ _ _

4. d y r
   d _ _ _

5. d k i n r
   d _ _ _ _ _

3. Look at the pictures and write the correct words.

| dog | mouse | cat | puppy | kitten |

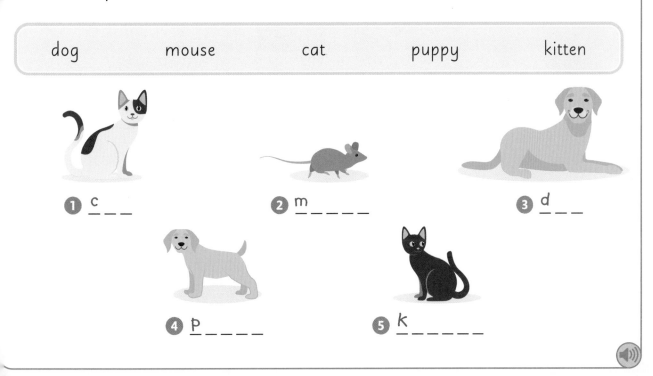

1 c _ _ _

2 m _ _ _ _ _

3 d _ _ _

4 p _ _ _ _ _

5 k _ _ _ _ _ _

4. Look at the pictures and circle the correct words.

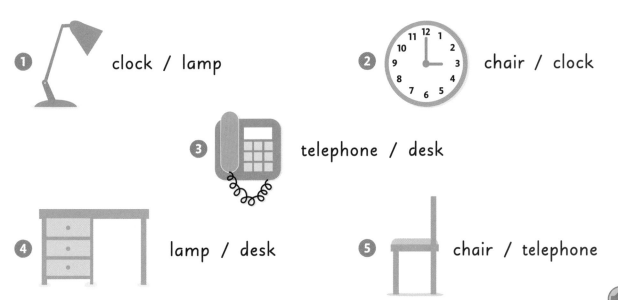

1 clock / lamp

2 chair / clock

3 telephone / desk

4 lamp / desk

5 chair / telephone

Week 17

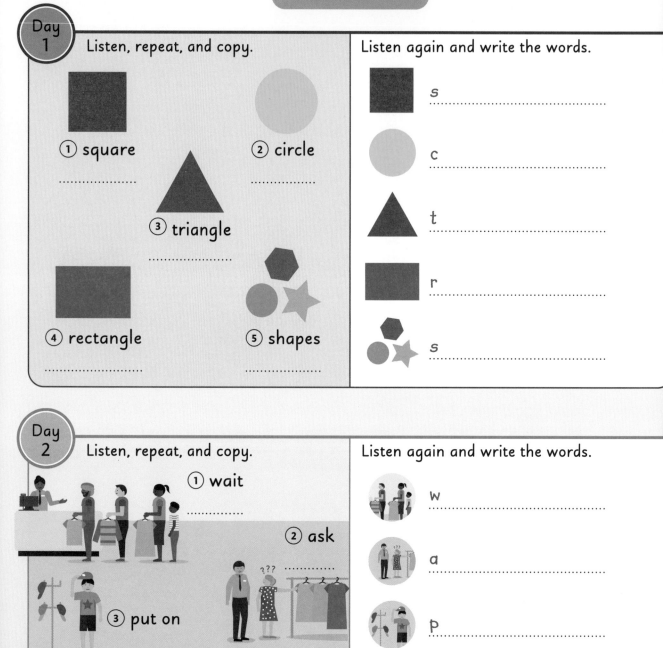

Day 1

Listen, repeat, and copy.

① square
② circle
③ triangle
④ rectangle
⑤ shapes

Listen again and write the words.

s
c
t
r
s

Day 2

Listen, repeat, and copy.

① wait
② ask
③ put on
④ choose
⑤ shop

Listen again and write the words.

w
a
p
c
s

Listen again and write the words.

d ....

c ....

b ....

l ....

a ....

Listen, repeat, and copy.

① dragonfly

....

② caterpillar

....

③ bee

....

④ ladybug

....

⑤ ant

....

Listen again and write the words.

w ....

j ....

l ....

m ....

d ....

Listen, repeat, and copy.

① water

....

② juice

....

③ lemonade

....

④ milkshake

....

⑤ drinks

....

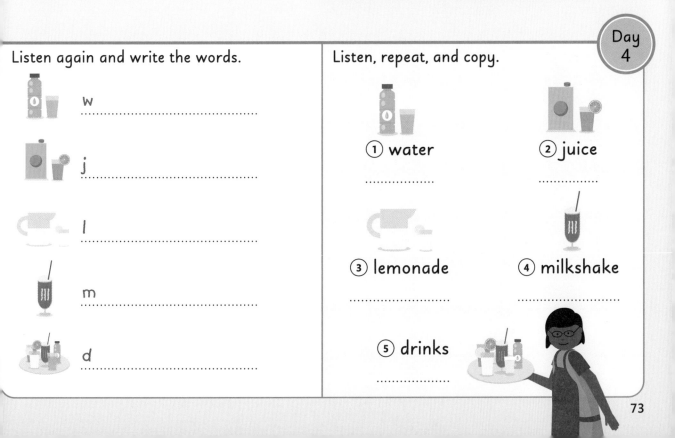

Day 5

What can you remember from this week?

1. Match the pictures to the correct words.

1. wait

2. ask

3. shop

4. choose

5. put on

2. Look at the pictures and check the correct words.

1.
bee ☐
ladybug ☐
dragonfly ☐

2.
caterpillar ☐
ant ☐
bee ☐

3.
ant ☐
dragonfly ☐
ladybug ☐

4.
caterpillar ☐
bee ☐
dragonfly ☐

5.
ladybug ☐
caterpillar ☐
ant ☐

3. Look at the pictures and write the correct words.

| water | juice | drinks | milkshake | lemonade |

1 j _ _ _ _

2 d _ _ _ _ _

3 w _ _ _ _ _

4 l _ _ _ _ _ _ _ _

5 m _ _ _ _ _ _ _ _ _

4. Look at the pictures and fill in the missing letters.

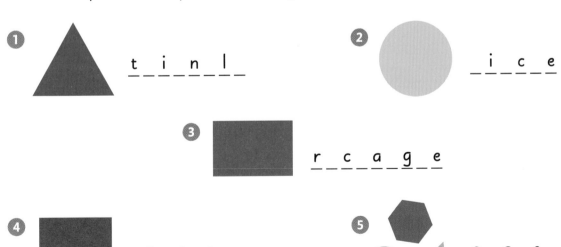

1 t _ i _ n _ l _

2 _ i _ c _ e

3 r _ c _ a _ g _ e

4 _ q _ a _ e

5 s _ a _ e _

75

Day 1

Listen, repeat, and copy.

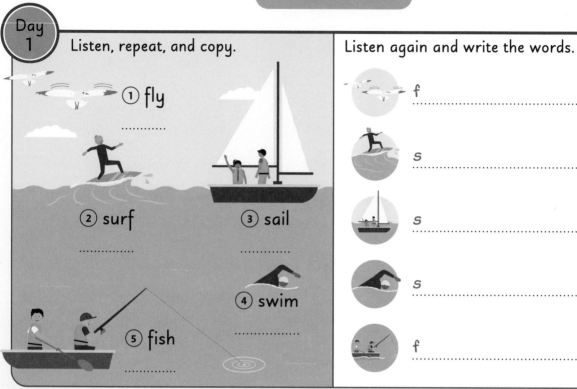

① fly

② surf

③ sail

④ swim

⑤ fish

Listen again and write the words.

f ....

s ....

s ....

s ....

f ....

Day 2

Listen, repeat, and copy.

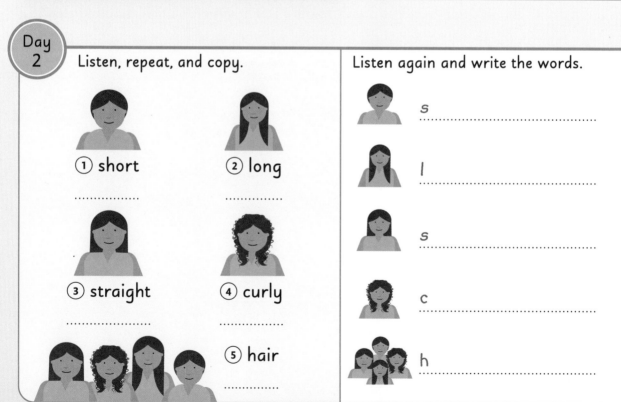

① short

② long

③ straight

④ curly

⑤ hair

Listen again and write the words.

s ....

l ....

s ....

c ....

h ....

Listen again and write the words.

v ....

f ....

d ....

n ....

p ....

Listen, repeat, and copy.

① vet

② firefighter

③ doctor

④ nurse

⑤ police officer

Listen again and write the words.

g ....

p ....

c ....

f ....

g ....

Listen, repeat, and copy.

① group

② parent

③ child

④ friends

⑤ grown-up

What can you remember from this week?

1. Read the words and check the correct pictures.

① vet

A ☐   B ☐

② firefighter

A ☐   B ☐

③ doctor

A ☐   B ☐

④ police officer

A ☐   B ☐

⑤ nurse

A ☐   B ☐

2. Look at the picture and write the correct words.

long

curly

hair

short

straight

① h _ _ _

② s _ _ _ _ _

③ l _ _ _ _

④ s _ _ _ _ _ _ _ _

⑤ c _ _ _ _

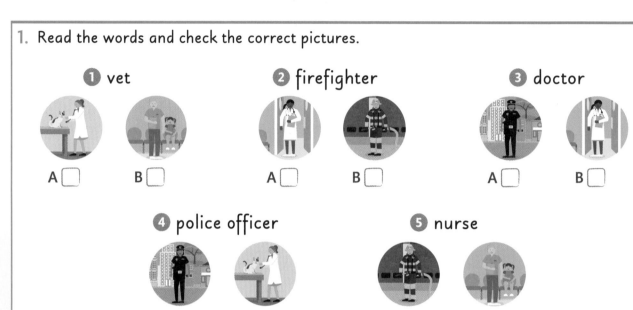

3. Look at the pictures and write the letters in the correct order.

s r f u

s _ _ _

f s h i

f _ _ _

f y l

f _ _

s m i w

s _ _ _

s l a i

s _ _ _

4. Look at the pictures and circle the correct words.

parent

child

grown-up

group

friends

parent

child

group

friends

grown-up

Day 1

Listen, repeat, and copy.

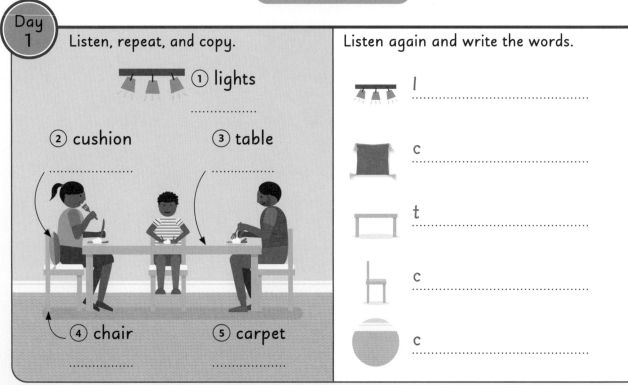

① lights

② cushion

③ table

④ chair

⑤ carpet

Listen again and write the words.

l ....

c ....

t ....

c ....

c ....

Day 2

Listen, repeat, and copy.

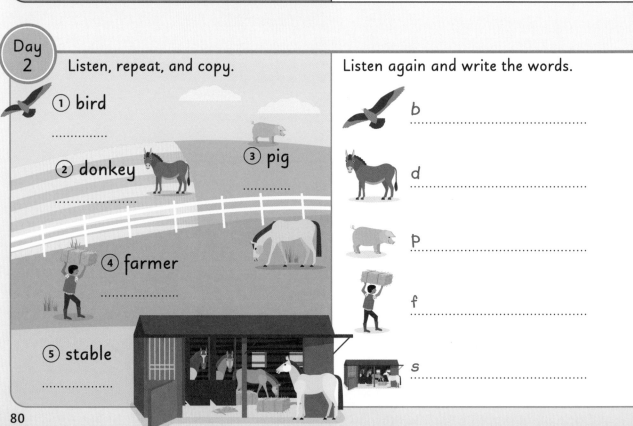

① bird

② donkey

③ pig

④ farmer

⑤ stable

Listen again and write the words.

b ....

d ....

p ....

f ....

s ....

Week 19

Listen again and write the words.

c ....

w ....

m ....

t ....

w ....

Listen, repeat, and copy.

① clap
....

② wave
....

③ move
....

④ touch
....

⑤ walk
....

Listen again and write the words.

b ....

p ....

c ....

c ....

c ....

Listen, repeat, and copy.

① birthday party
....

② present
....

③ candle
....

④ card
....

⑤ cake
....

Day
5

What can you remember from this week?

1. Match the pictures to the correct words.

clap

move

walk

wave

touch

2. Look at the pictures and write the correct words.

bird   donkey   stable
farmer   pig

1   b _ _ _

2   d _ _ _ _ _

3   s _ _ _ _ _

4   p _ _

5   f _ _ _ _ _

3. Look at the pictures and circle the correct words.

 **1** present / birthday party

 **2** card / candle

 **3** cake / birthday party

 **4** candle / present

 **5** card / cake

4. Look at the pictures and write the correct words.

 **1** c _ _ _ _ _

 **2** c _ _ _ _ _ _

 **3** l _ _ _ _ _

4 c _ _ _ _

5 t _ _ _ _

Week 20

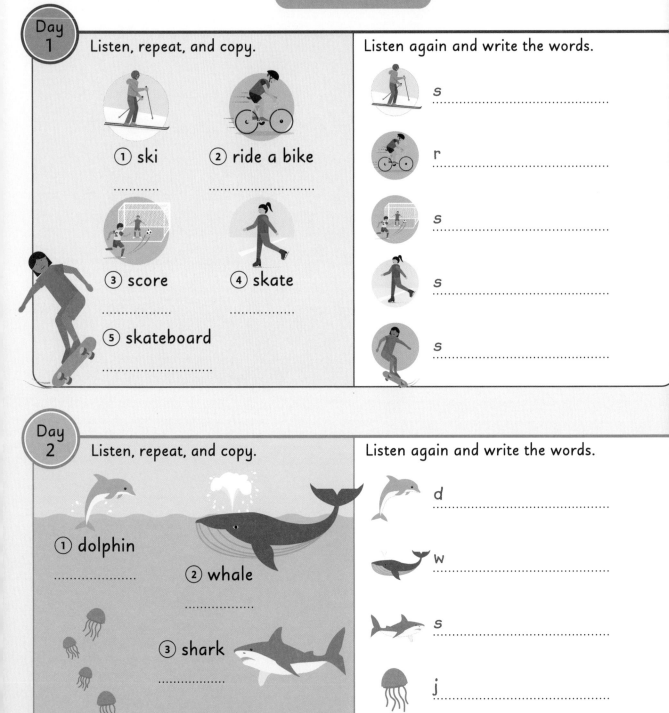

Day 1

Listen, repeat, and copy.

① ski ② ride a bike

③ score ④ skate

⑤ skateboard

Listen again and write the words.

s ....

r ....

s ....

s ....

s ....

Day 2

Listen, repeat, and copy.

① dolphin

② whale

③ shark

④ jellyfish ⑤ octopus

Listen again and write the words.

d ....

w ....

s ....

j ....

o ....

Listen again and write the words.

s ....

h ....

c ....

e ....

f ....

Listen, repeat, and copy.

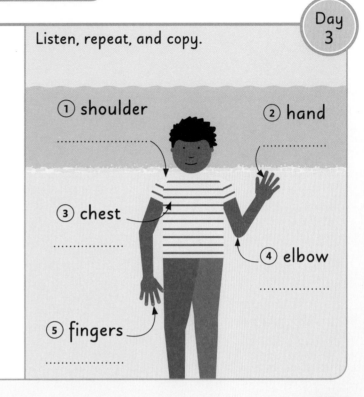

① shoulder

....

② hand

....

③ chest

....

④ elbow

....

⑤ fingers

....

Listen again and write the words.

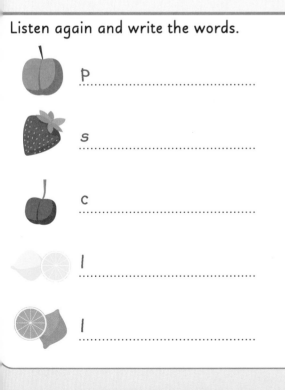

p ....

s ....

c ....

l ....

l ....

Listen, repeat, and copy.

① peach

....

② strawberry

....

③ cherry

....

④ lemon

....

⑤ lime

....

85

Day 5

What can you remember from this week?

---

1. Read the words and check the correct pictures.

① score

A ☐   B ☐

② skate

A ☐   B ☐

③ ski

A ☐   B ☐

④ ride a bike

A ☐   B ☐

⑤ skateboard

A ☐   B ☐

---

2. Look at the pictures and fill in the missing letters.

① <u>d _ l _ h _ n</u>

② <u>j _ l _ y _ i _ h</u>

③ <u>o _ t _ p _ s</u>

④ <u>s _ a _ k</u>

⑤ <u>w _ a _ e</u>

3. Match the pictures to the correct words.

 1

shoulder

 2

hand

 3

fingers

 4

chest

 5

elbow

4. Look at the pictures and write the correct words.

lime cherry peach
lemon strawberry

1  l _ _ _ _

2  c _ _ _ _ _

3  s _ _ _ _ _ _ _ _ _

4  p _ _ _ _

5 l _ _ _

Week 21

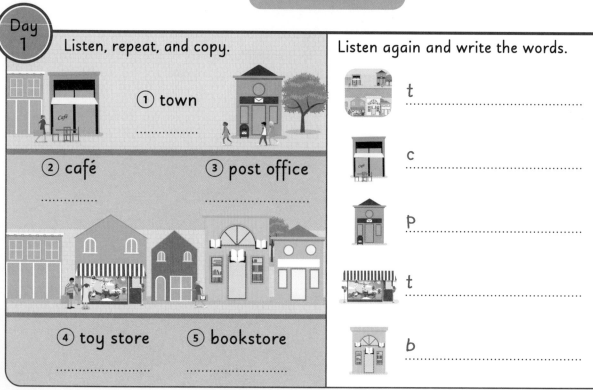

Day 1

Listen, repeat, and copy.

① town

② café   ③ post office

④ toy store   ⑤ bookstore

Listen again and write the words.

t ....

c ....

p ....

t ....

b ....

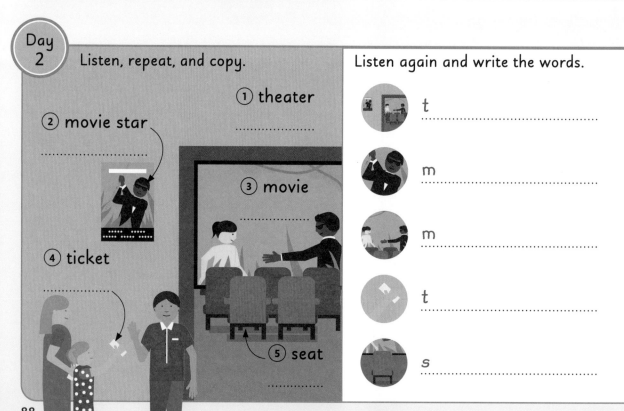

Day 2

Listen, repeat, and copy.

① theater

② movie star

③ movie

④ ticket

⑤ seat

Listen again and write the words.

t ....

m ....

m ....

t ....

s ....

Week 21

Listen again and write the words.

t ....

e ....

e- ....

m ....

a ....

Listen, repeat, and copy.

① tablet

....

② email

....

③ e-book

....

④ message

....

⑤ apps

....

Listen again and write the words.

s ....

s ....

s ....

b ....

b ....

Listen, repeat, and copy.

① swing

....

② seesaw

....

③ slide

....

④ bench

....

⑤ bicycle

....

Week 21

Day 5

What can you remember from this week?

1. Look at the pictures and write the correct words.

❶    t _ _ _ _ _ _

❷    e - _ _ _ _ _ _

❸    m _ _ _ _ _ _ _

❹    a _ _ _

❺    e _ _ _ _

2. Match the pictures to the correct words.

❶    post office

❷    café

❸    bookstore

❹    town

❺   toy store

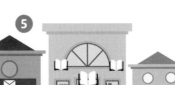

3. Look at the pictures and circle the correct words.

 seat / theater

 movie / theater

 movie star / seat

 ticket / movie star

 movie star / seat

ticket / movie star

ticket / movie

4. Read the words and check the correct pictures.

1 bicycle

A ☐   B ☐

2 swing

A ☐   B ☐

3 bench

A ☐   B ☐

4 seesaw

A ☐   B ☐

5 slide

A ☐   B ☐

91

Day 1

Listen, repeat, and copy.

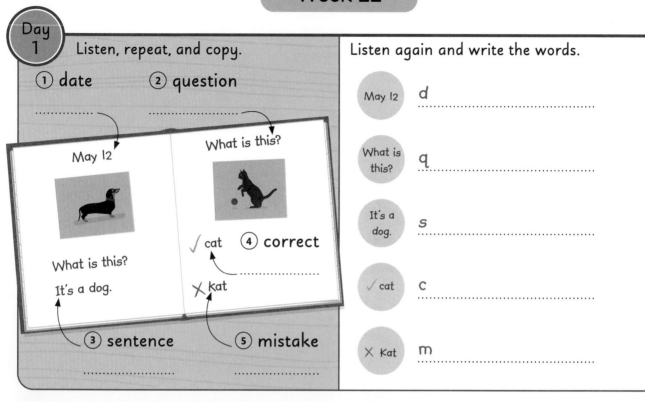

① date
② question
③ sentence
④ correct
⑤ mistake

May 12
What is this?
It's a dog.
What is this?
✓ cat
✗ kat

Listen again and write the words.

May 12	d ....
What is this?	q ....
It's a dog.	s ....
✓ cat	c ....
✗ Kat	m ....

Day 2

Listen, repeat, and copy.

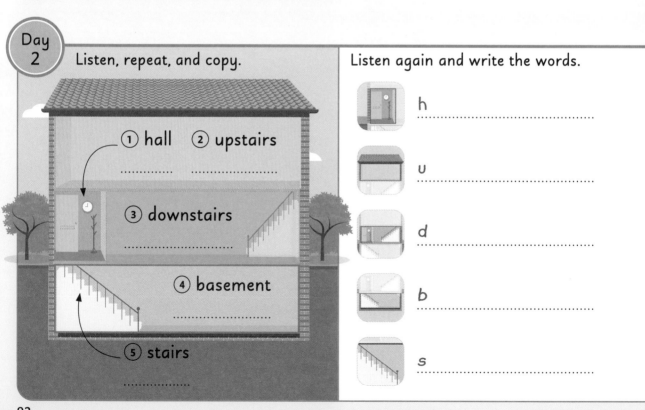

① hall
② upstairs
③ downstairs
④ basement
⑤ stairs

Listen again and write the words.

h ....
u ....
d ....
b ....
s ....

Week 22

Listen again and write the words.

c ....

r ....

d ....

t ....

p ....

Listen, repeat, and copy.

① clean

....

② relax

....

③ do homework

....

④ tidy

....

⑤ practice

....

Listen again and write the words.

s ....

s ....

g ....

t ....

s ....

Listen, repeat, and copy.

① swimming pool

....

② swimming

....

③ goggles

....

④ towel

....

⑤ swimsuit

....

Week 22

What can you remember from this week?

1. Look at the picture and write the correct words.

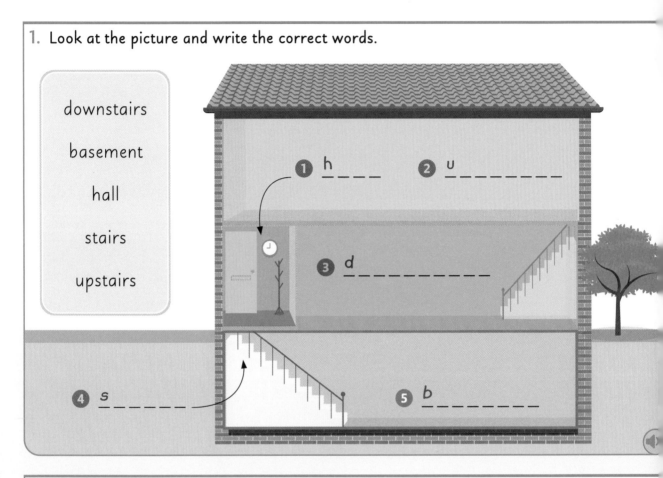

downstairs

basement

hall

stairs

upstairs

❶ h _ _ _ _   ❷ u _ _ _ _ _ _ _ _

❸ d _ _ _ _ _ _ _ _ _ _

❹ s _ _ _ _ _ _ _   ❺ b _ _ _ _ _ _ _

2. Match the pictures to the correct words.

tidy   relax   do homework   clean   practice

3. Look at the pictures and circle the correct words.

1 swimming pool
   towel

2 goggles
   swimming pool

3 swimsuit
   towel

4 goggles
   swimming

5 swimming
   swimsuit

4. Look at the pictures and fill in the missing letters.

1 ✓ cat   c _ _ e _ t

2 What is   q _ e _ t _ o _
   this?

3 May 12   _ a _ e

4 ✗ Kat   m _ s _ a _ e

5 It's a   _ e _ t _ n _ e
   dog.

Day 1

Listen, repeat, and copy.

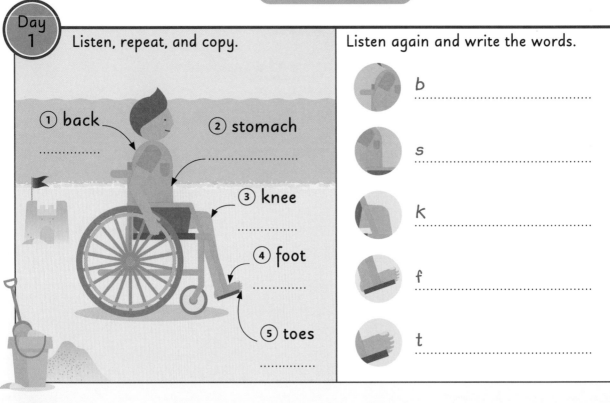

① back

② stomach

③ knee

④ foot

⑤ toes

Listen again and write the words.

b ....

s ....

k ....

f ....

t ....

Day 2

Listen, repeat, and copy.

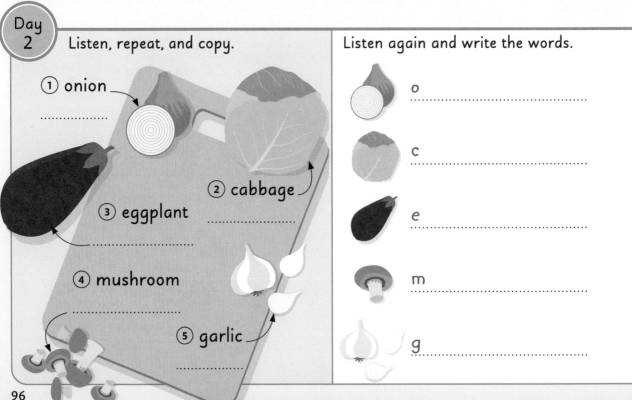

① onion

② cabbage

③ eggplant

④ mushroom

⑤ garlic

Listen again and write the words.

o ....

c ....

e ....

m ....

g ....

Listen again and write the words.

g ....

v ....

t ....

s ....

g ....

Listen, repeat, and copy.

① golf

....

② volleyball

....

③ table tennis

....

④ soccer

....

⑤ gymnastics

....

Listen again and write the words.

w ....

c ....

r ....

l ....

t ....

Listen, repeat, and copy.

① waterfall

....

② cave

....

③ river

....

④ lizard

....

⑤ tortoise

....

Day 5

What can you remember from this week?

1. Look at the pictures and check the correct words.

 **1**

onion ☐
cabbage ☐

 **2**

mushroom ☐
garlic ☐

 **3**

cabbage ☐
eggplant ☐

 4

onion ☐
mushroom ☐

 **5**

garlic ☐
eggplant ☐

2. Look at the pictures and write the correct words.

 1

r _ _ _ _ _

 2

w _ _ _ _ _ _ _ _

 3

c _ _ _ _

 **4**

l _ _ _ _ _ _

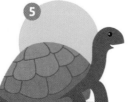 **5**

t _ _ _ _ _ _ _

Week 23

3. Look at the pictures and circle the correct words.

 golf / gymnastics

 volleyball / soccer

 table tennis / gymnastics

 volleyball / table tennis

 soccer / golf

4. Look at the picture and write the correct words.

foot

knee

stomach

back

toes

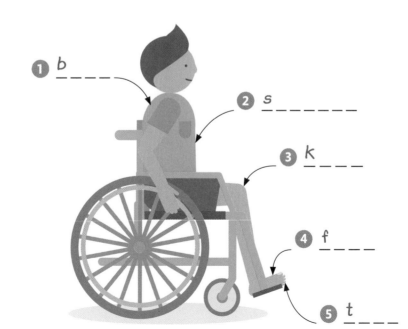

1 b _ _ _ _

2 s _ _ _ _ _ _ _

3 k _ _ _ _

4 f _ _ _ _

5 t _ _ _ _

Week 24

Day 1

Listen, repeat, and copy.

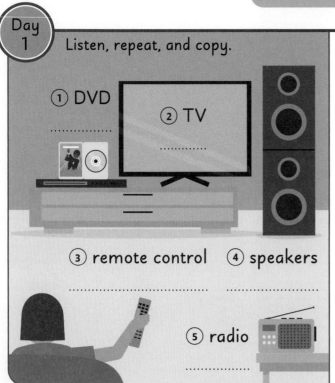

① DVD

② TV

③ remote control ④ speakers

⑤ radio

Listen again and write the words.

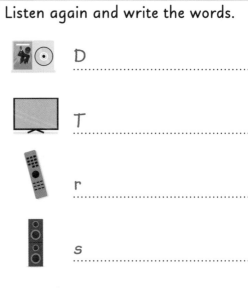

D..................................

T..................................

r..................................

s..................................

r..................................

Day 2

Listen, repeat, and copy.

① phone

② email

③ send

④ talk

⑤ shout

Listen again and write the words.

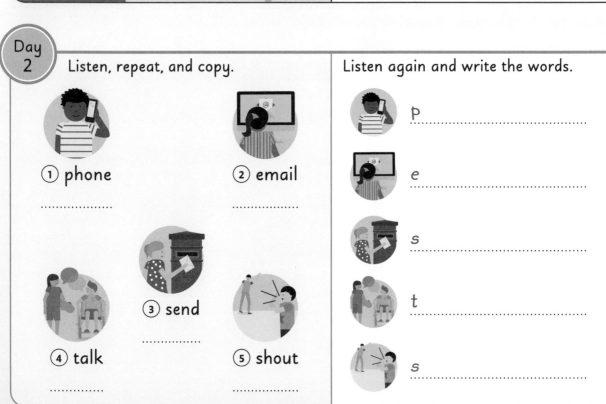

p..................................

e..................................

s..................................

t..................................

s..................................

100

Listen again and write the words.

d ....

p ....

c ....

c ....

s ....

Listen, repeat, and copy.

① desert
....

② pyramid
....

③ camel
....

④ crocodile
....

⑤ snake
....

Listen again and write the words.

b ....

b ....

d ....

p ....

t ....

Listen, repeat, and copy.

① bus station
....

② bus
....

③ driver
....

④ passenger
....

⑤ taxi
....

Day 5

What can you remember from this week?

1. Read the words and check the correct pictures.

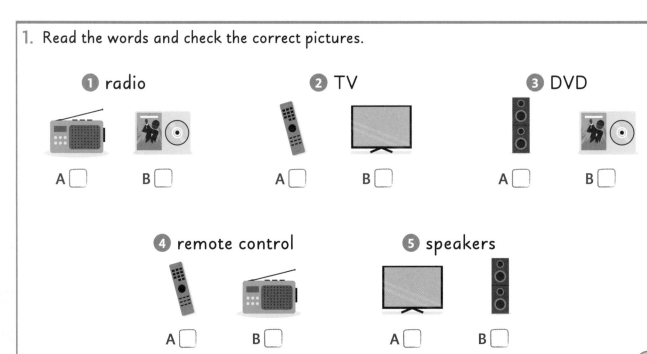

① radio

A ☐   B ☐

② TV

A ☐   B ☐

③ DVD

A ☐   B ☐

④ remote control

A ☐   B ☐

⑤ speakers

A ☐   B ☐

2. Look at the pictures and write the correct words.

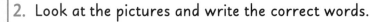

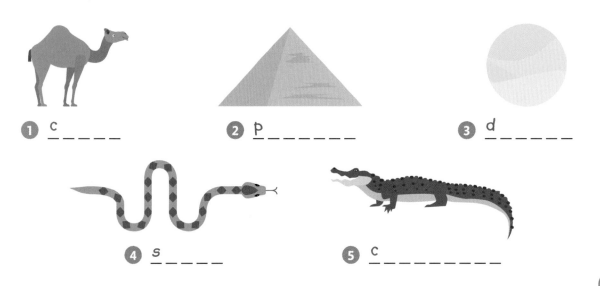

① c _ _ _ _

② p _ _ _ _ _ _

③ d _ _ _ _ _

④ s _ _ _ _ _

⑤ c _ _ _ _ _ _ _ _

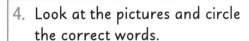

Week 24

3. Match the pictures to the correct words.

 passenger

 taxi

 bus station

 bus

 driver

4. Look at the pictures and circle the correct words.

 send / phone

 email / shout

 talk / send

 phone / shout

 talk / email

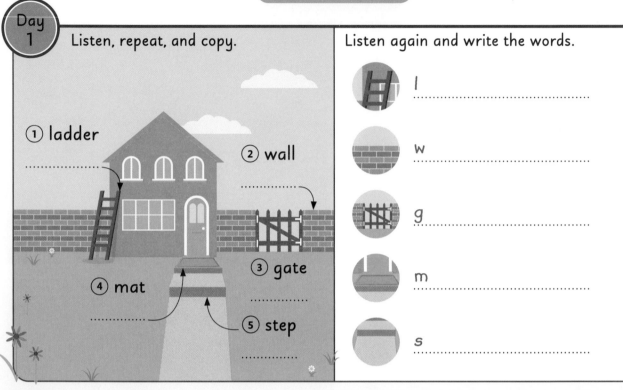

Day 1

Listen, repeat, and copy.

1. ladder
2. wall
3. gate
4. mat
5. step

Listen again and write the words.

l ....

w ....

g ....

m ....

s ....

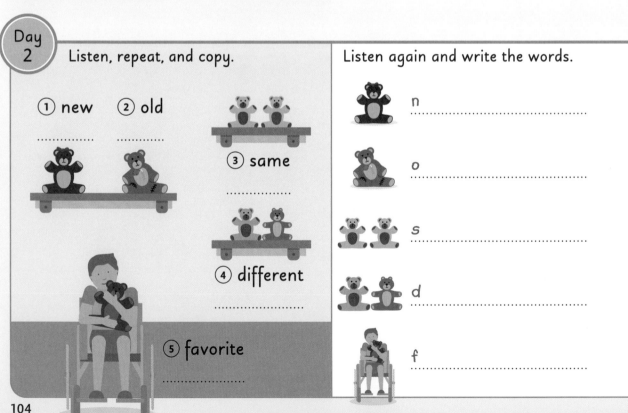

Day 2

Listen, repeat, and copy.

1. new
2. old
3. same
4. different
5. favorite

Listen again and write the words.

n ....

o ....

s ....

d ....

f ....

Listen again and write the words.

+ a ....

t ....

m ....

f ....

c ....

Listen, repeat, and copy.

① ambulance   ② truck

....

③ motorcycle

....

④ fire engine

....

⑤ car

....

Listen again and write the words.

d ....

w ....

m ....

b ....

g ....

Listen, repeat, and copy.

① dream   ② wake up

....

③ make the bed   ④ brush my teeth

....

⑤ get dressed

....

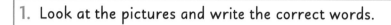

Week 25

Day 5   What can you remember from this week?

1. Look at the pictures and write the correct words.

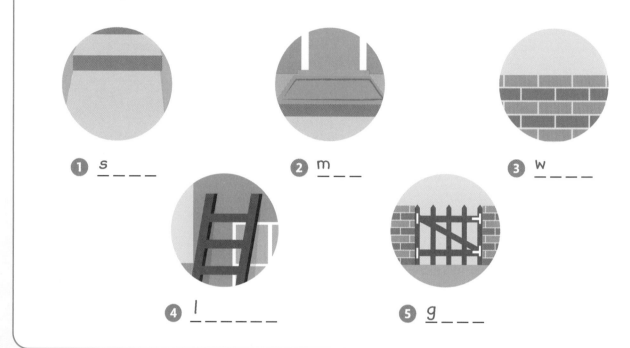

1 s _ _ _ _

2 m _ _ _

3 w _ _ _ _

4 l _ _ _ _ _ _

5 g _ _ _ _

2. Match the pictures to the correct words.

truck   car   ambulance   motorcycle   fire engine

Read the words and check the correct pictures.

1 wake up   A ☐   B ☐

2 make the bed   A ☐   B ☐

3 brush my teeth   A ☐   B ☐

4 get dressed   A ☐   B ☐

5 dream   A ☐   B ☐

4. Look at the pictures and fill in the missing letters.

1    s _ _ m _

2    d _ f _ e _ e _ t

3    n _ _ w

4    f _ v _ r _ t _

5    o _ _ d

107

Week 26

Day 1

Listen, repeat, and copy.

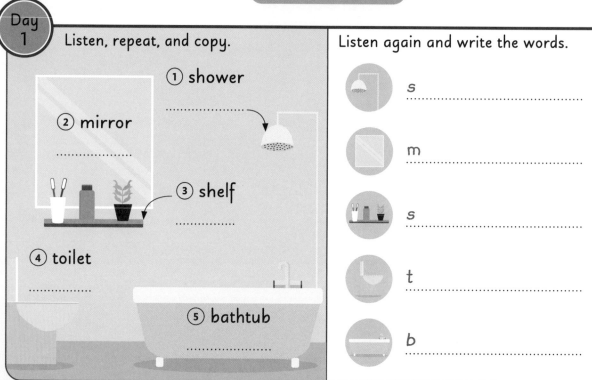

① shower

② mirror

③ shelf

④ toilet

⑤ bathtub

Listen again and write the words.

s ....

m ....

s ....

t ....

b ....

Day 2

Listen, repeat, and copy.

① gorilla

② panda

③ rhino

④ parrot

⑤ kangaroo

Listen again and write the words.

g ....

p ....

r ....

p ....

k ....

Listen again and write the words.

f ....

h ....

c ....

h ....

t ....

Listen, repeat, and copy.

① fall over   ② hurt   ③ cry

....

④ help   ⑤ tell

....

Listen again and write the words.

s ....

c ....

s ....

g ....

b ....

Listen, repeat, and copy.

① scarf
....

② coat
....

③ sweater
....

④ gloves
....

⑤ boots
....

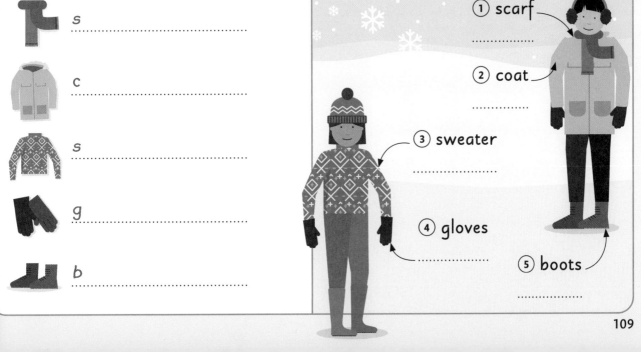

Day
5

What can you remember from this week?

1. Look at the pictures and write the correct words.

1. t _ _ _ _

2. c _ _ _

3. h _ _ _ _

4. h _ _ _

5. f _ _ _ _ _ _ _ _

2. Look at the pictures and check the correct words.

1.
rhino ☐
kangaroo ☐
parrot ☐

2.
gorilla ☐
panda ☐
rhino ☐

3.
parrot ☐
rhino ☐
gorilla ☐

4.
kangaroo ☐
gorilla ☐
panda ☐

5.
panda ☐
parrot ☐
kangaroo ☐

3. Look at the pictures and write the correct words.

| coat | boots | gloves | scarf | sweater |

1 b _ _ _ _ _

2 s _ _ _ _ _ _ _

3 s _ _ _ _ _

4 c _ _ _ _

5 g _ _ _ _ _ _

4. Look at the pictures and circle the correct words.

1 shower / bathtub

2 toilet / shelf

3 bathtub / mirror

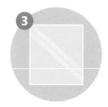
4 mirror / shelf

5 shower / toilet

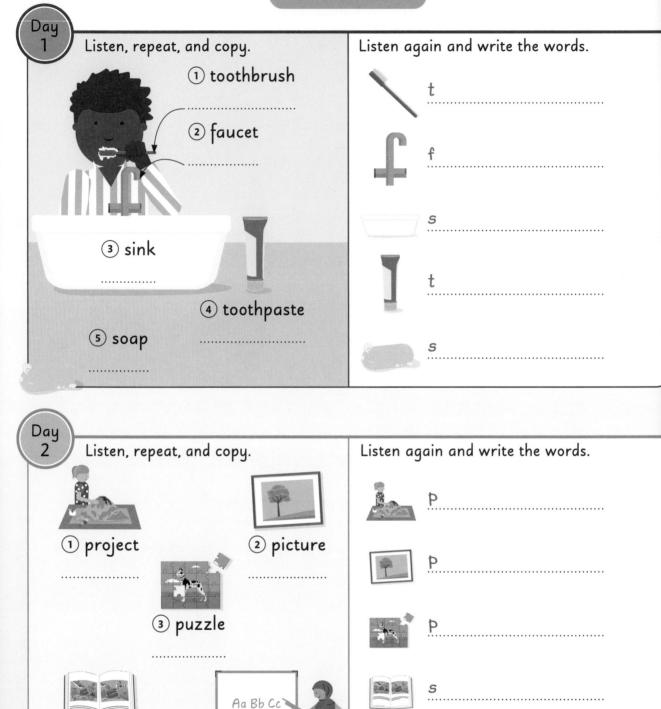

Day 1

Listen, repeat, and copy.

① toothbrush

② faucet

③ sink

④ toothpaste

⑤ soap

Listen again and write the words.

t

f

s

t

s

Day 2

Listen, repeat, and copy.

① project

② picture

③ puzzle

④ story

⑤ lesson

Aa Bb Cc

Listen again and write the words.

p

p

p

s

l

Listen again and write the words.

s ....

e ....

f ....

t ....

h ....

Listen, repeat, and copy.

① scared

② excited

③ friendly

④ thirsty

⑤ hungry

Listen again and write the words.

m ....

l ....

c ....

f ....

b ....

Listen, repeat, and copy.

① mountain

② lake

③ castle

④ forest

⑤ boat

Day 5

What can you remember from this week?

1. Look at the pictures and write the letters in the correct order.

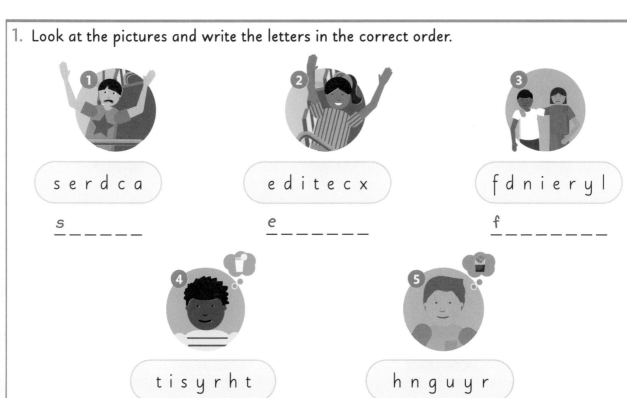

1

s e r d c a

s _ _ _ _ _

2

e d i t e c x

e _ _ _ _ _ _

3

f d n i e r y l

f _ _ _ _ _ _ _

4

t i s y r h t

t _ _ _ _ _ _

5

h n g u y r

h _ _ _ _ _

2. Match the pictures to the correct words.

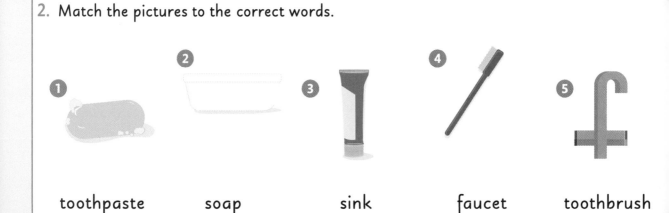

1   2   3   4   5

toothpaste   soap   sink   faucet   toothbrush

3. Look at the pictures and check the correct words.

 project ☐
picture ☐

 story ☐
puzzle ☐

 lesson ☐
picture ☐

 story ☐
project ☐

 puzzle ☐
lesson ☐

4. Look at the pictures and fill in the missing letters.

 f _ r _ s _

 _ o _ n _ a _ n

 c _ s _ l _

 _ a _ e

 b _ _ a _

Week 28

Day 1

Listen, repeat, and copy.

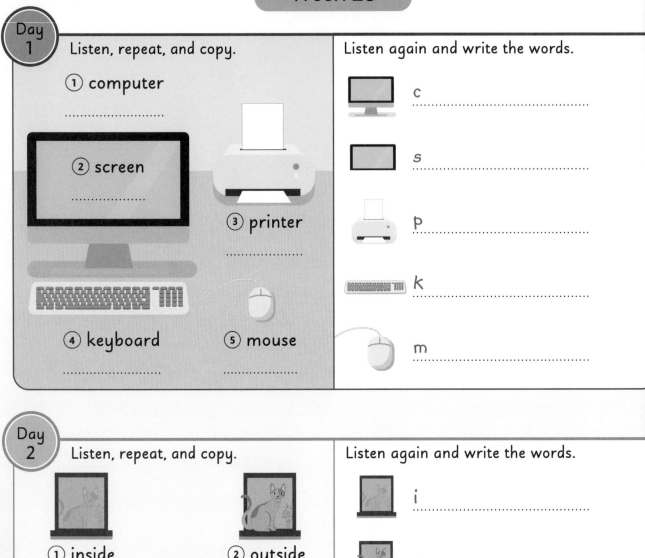

① computer

....

② screen

....

③ printer

....

④ keyboard

....

⑤ mouse

....

Listen again and write the words.

c ....

s ....

p ....

k ....

m ....

Day 2

Listen, repeat, and copy.

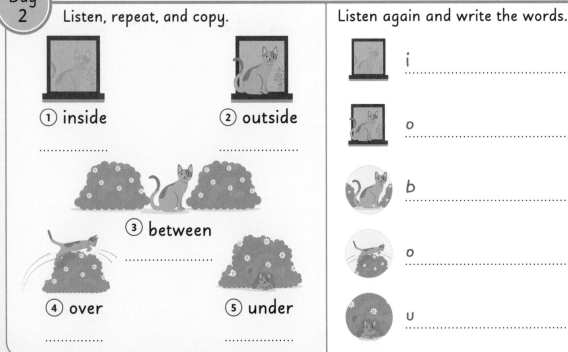

① inside

....

② outside

....

③ between

....

④ over

....

⑤ under

....

Listen again and write the words.

i ....

o ....

b ....

o ....

u ....

116

Listen again and write the words.

w ....

f ....

c ....

s ....

w ....

Listen, repeat, and copy.

① weather

② foggy

③ cloudy

④ sunny

⑤ windy

Listen again and write the words.

c ....

c ....

r ....

i ....

c ....

Listen, repeat, and copy.

① carnival

② circus

③ ride

④ ice cream

⑤ clown

Day 5

What can you remember from this week?

1. Read the words and check the correct pictures.

① inside   A ☐   B ☐

② outside   A ☐   B ☐

③ between   A ☐   B ☐

④ over   A ☐   B ☐

⑤ under   A ☐   B ☐

2. Look at the pictures and write the correct words.

①   f _ _ _ _ _

②   s _ _ _ _ _

③   w _ _ _ _ _ _ _

④   w _ _ _ _ _

⑤    c _ _ _ _ _ _

3. Look at the pictures and circle the correct words.

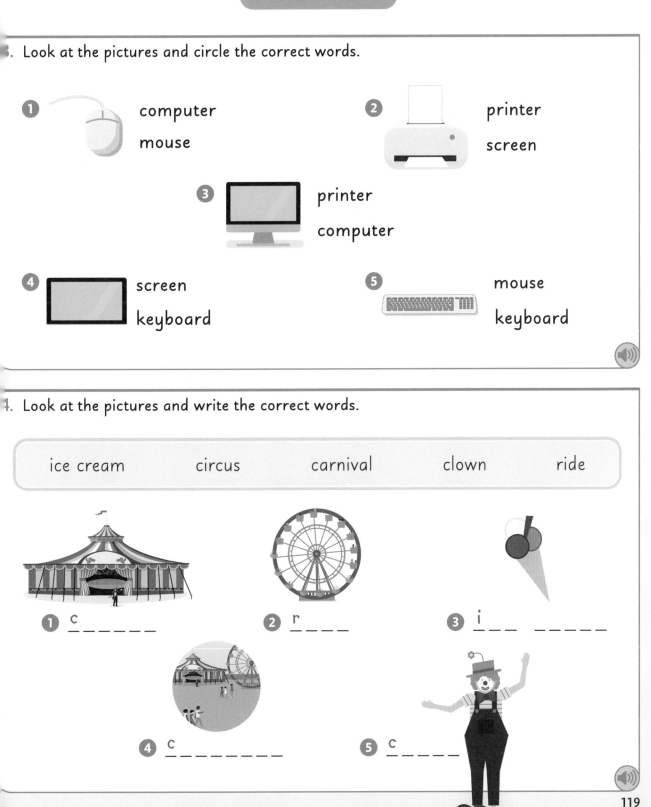

1. computer
   mouse

2. printer
   screen

3. printer
   computer

4. screen
   keyboard

5. mouse
   keyboard

4. Look at the pictures and write the correct words.

| ice cream | circus | carnival | clown | ride |

1. c _ _ _ _ _ _

2. r _ _ _ _

3. i _ _ _   _ _ _ _ _

4. c _ _ _ _ _ _ _ _

5. c _ _ _ _ _

Day 1

Listen, repeat, and copy.

① soup

② pie

③ rice

④ beans

⑤ meat

Listen again and write the words.

s ....

p ....

r ....

b ....

m ....

Day 2

Listen, repeat, and copy.

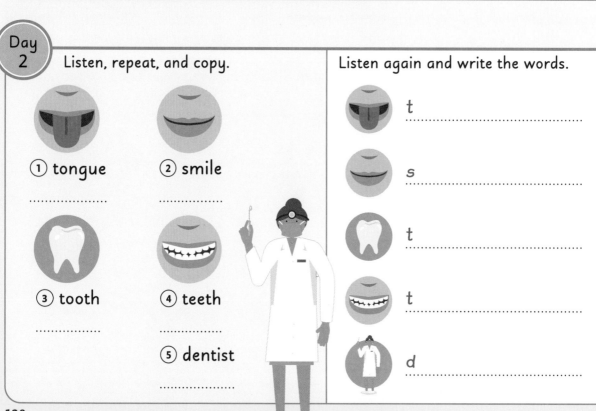

① tongue

② smile

③ tooth

④ teeth

⑤ dentist

Listen again and write the words.

t ....

s ....

t ....

t ....

d ....

Listen again and write the words.

s ....

f ....

t ....

j ....

c ....

Listen, repeat, and copy.

① search

....

② find

....

③ try

....

④ join

....

⑤ complete

....

Listen again and write the words.

f ....

l ....

f ....

f ....

n ....

Listen, repeat, and copy.

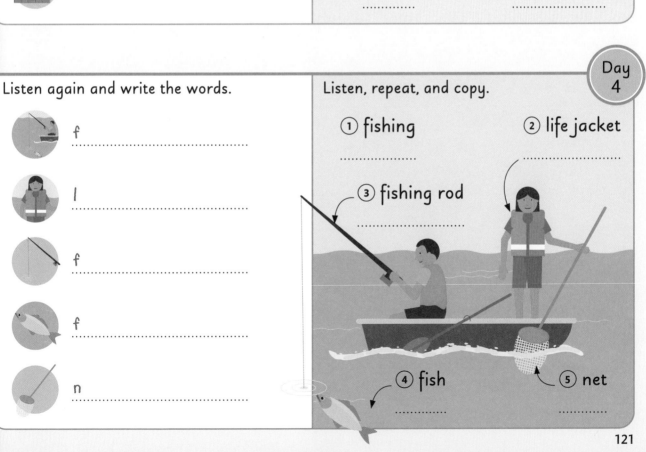

① fishing

....

② life jacket

....

③ fishing rod

....

④ fish

....

⑤ net

....

Day 5

What can you remember from this week?

1. Look at the pictures and fill in the missing letters.

① s e _ r _ h

② f _ _ n _

③ j _ _ i _

④ c _ m _ l _ t

⑤ _ _ r _

2. Match the pictures to the correct words.

①

②

③

④

⑤

fishing   fish   life jacket   fishing rod   net

3. Look at the pictures and write the correct words.

1. t _ _ _ _

2. t _ _ _ _ _ _

3. t _ _ _ _

4. s _ _ _ _

5. d _ _ _ _ _ _

4. Look at the pictures and check the correct words.

1. soup ☐
   beans ☐
   rice ☐

2. meat ☐
   pie ☐
   beans ☐

3. rice ☐
   soup ☐
   pie ☐

4. beans ☐
   meat ☐
   soup ☐

5. pie ☐
   rice ☐
   meat ☐

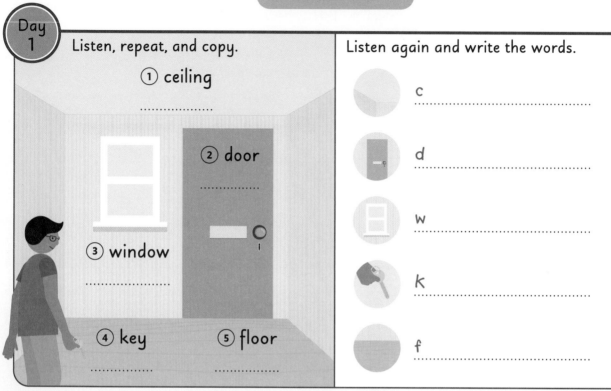

Day 1

Listen, repeat, and copy.

① ceiling

....

② door

....

③ window

....

④ key   ⑤ floor

....

Listen again and write the words.

c ....

d ....

w ....

k ....

f ....

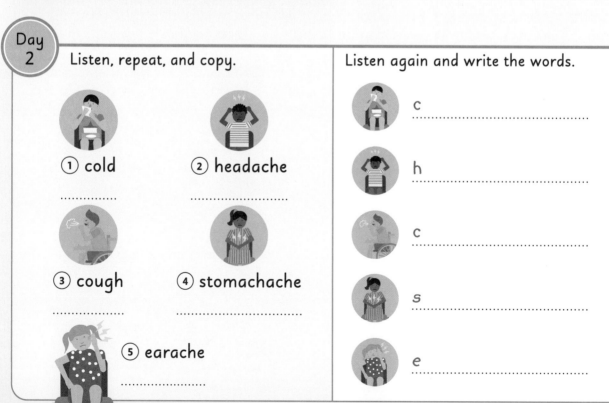

Day 2

Listen, repeat, and copy.

① cold   ② headache

....

③ cough   ④ stomachache

....

⑤ earache

....

Listen again and write the words.

c ....

h ....

c ....

s ....

e ....

124

Week 30

Listen again and write the words.

l ....

s ....

e ....

n ....

a ....

Listen, repeat, and copy.

① letter

② stamp

③ envelope

④ name

Sofia

10 Park Street
New York,
NY 10018

⑤ address

Listen again and write the words.

c ....

h ....

v ....

w ....

m ....

Listen, repeat, and copy.

① countryside

② hills

③ village

④ woods

⑤ market

Day 5

What can you remember from this week?

1. Look at the pictures and write the correct words.

> hills   village   woods
> countryside   market

1. v _ _ _ _ _ _

2. h _ _ _ _

3. c _ _ _ _ _ _ _ _ _ _ _

4. w _ _ _ _

5. m _ _ _ _ _

2. Look at the pictures and check the correct words.

1. letter ☐
   stamp ☐

2. 10 Park Street New York, NY 10018
   name ☐
   address ☐

3. envelope ☐
   letter ☐

4. address ☐
   stamp ☐

5. Sofia
   envelope ☐
   name ☐

3. Read the words and check the correct pictures.

1 cold

A ☐   B ☐

2 headache

A ☐   B ☐

3 cough

A ☐   B ☐

4 earache

A ☐   B ☐

5 stomachache

A ☐   B ☐

4. Look at the pictures and write the correct words.

1 c _ _ _ _ _ _   **2** w _ _ _ _ _ _   **3** d _ _ _ _

4 f _ _ _ _ _   **5** k _ _ _

127

Day 1

Listen, repeat, and copy.

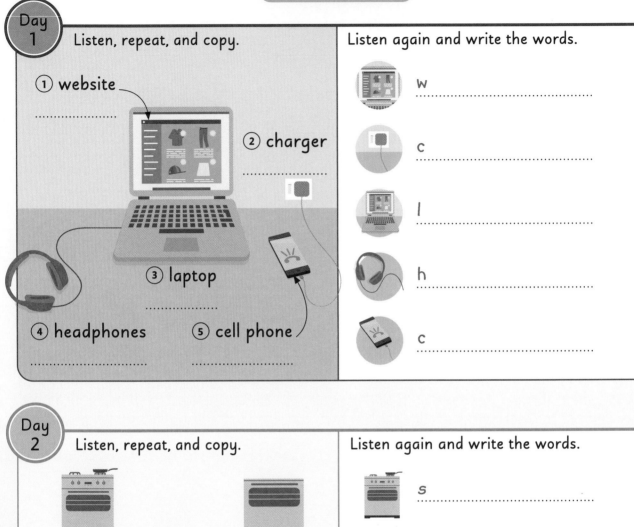

① website

② charger

③ laptop

④ headphones

⑤ cell phone

Listen again and write the words.

w ....

c ....

l ....

h ....

c ....

Day 2

Listen, repeat, and copy.

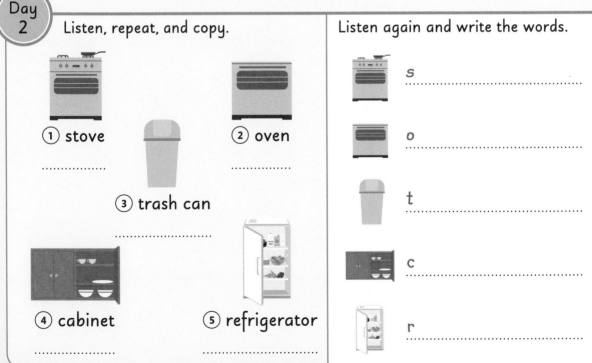

① stove

② oven

③ trash can

④ cabinet

⑤ refrigerator

Listen again and write the words.

s ....

o ....

t ....

c ....

r ....

Listen again and write the words.

s ....

s ....

g ....

l ....

o ....

Listen, repeat, and copy.

① stadium

....

② supermarket

....

③ gym

....

④ library

....

⑤ office

....

Listen again and write the words.

s ....

c ....

g ....

r ....

i ....

Listen, repeat, and copy.

① sky

....

② cloud

....

③ ground

....

④ rock

....

⑤ insects

....

Day 5

What can you remember from this week?

1. Read the words and check the correct pictures.

1 laptop

A ☐   B ☐

2 website

A ☐   B ☐

3 headphones

A ☐   B ☐

4 cell phone

A ☐   B ☐

5 charger

 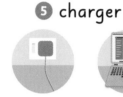

A ☐   B ☐

2. Look at the pictures and write the correct words.

1    o _ _ _ _ _ _

2    l _ _ _ _ _ _ _

3    s _ _ _ _ _ _ _

4    g _ _ _

5    s _ _ _ _ _ _ _ _ _ _ _

3. Look at the pictures and circle the correct words.

① stove

cabinet

② trash can

stove

③ oven

trash can

④ refrigerator

cabinet

⑤ oven

refrigerator

4. Look at the pictures and fill in the missing letters.

① r _ c _

② s _ _ y

③ c _ o _ d

④ g _ o _ n _

⑤ i _ s _ c _ s

Day 1

Listen, repeat, and copy.

① snowflake

② snowman

③ snowball

④ snow

⑤ ice

Listen again and write the words.

s ....

s ....

s ....

s ....

i ....

Day 2

Listen, repeat, and copy.

① hop

② turn

③ swing

④ play

⑤ whistle

Listen again and write the words.

h ....

t ....

s ....

p ....

w ....

Week 32

Listen again and write the words.

r.....................................

b.....................................

t.....................................

c.....................................

t.....................................

Listen, repeat, and copy.

① road

② bus stop
....

③ traffic
....

④ crosswalk
....

⑤ traffic lights
....

Listen again and write the words.

r.....................................

c.....................................

f.....................................

m.....................................

w.....................................

Listen, repeat, and copy.

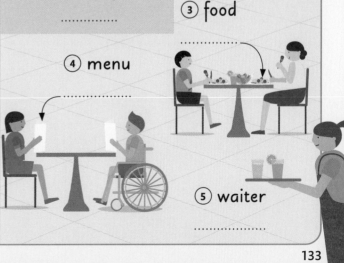

① restaurant
....

② chef
....

③ food
....

④ menu
....

⑤ waiter
....

Day 5

What can you remember from this week?

1. Read the words and check the correct pictures.

① snowman   A ☐   B ☐

② snow   A ☐   B ☐

③ snowflake   A ☐   B ☐

④ snowball   A ☐   B ☐

⑤ ice   A ☐   B ☐

2. Look at the pictures and write the correct words.

m _ _ _ _

r _ _ _ _ _ _ _ _ _

c _ _ _ _

f _ _ _ _

w _ _ _ _ _ _

Week 32

3. Look at the pictures and write the letters in the correct order.

p y a l

1 p _ _ _

h p o

2 h _ _

t r n u

3 t _ _ _

s n i w g

4 s _ _ _ _

w s t i l e h

5 w _ _ _ _ _ _

4. Match the pictures to the correct words.

traffic   crosswalk   road   traffic lights   bus stop

Day 1

Listen, repeat, and copy.

Listen again and write the words.

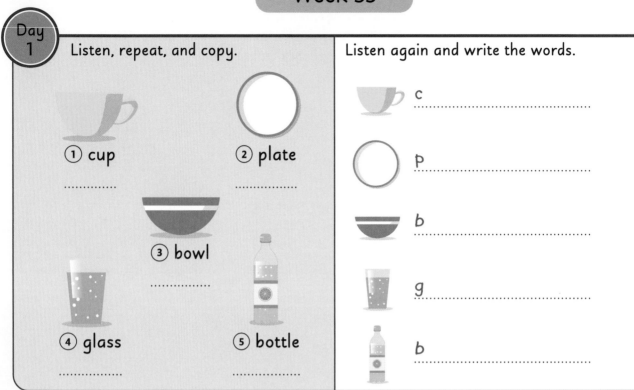

① cup

② plate

③ bowl

④ glass

⑤ bottle

c ....

p ....

b ....

g ....

b ....

Day 2

Listen, repeat, and copy.

Listen again and write the words.

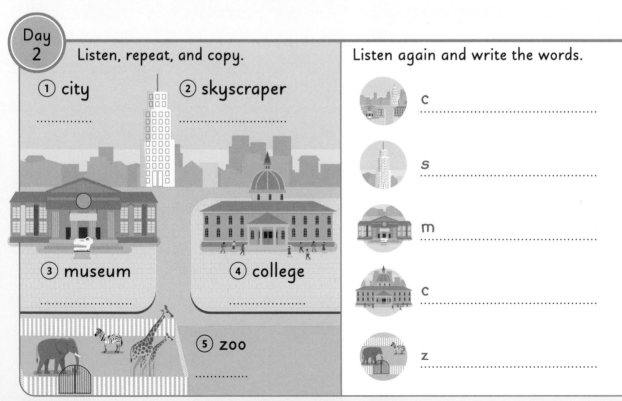

① city

② skyscraper

③ museum

④ college

⑤ zoo

c ....

s ....

m ....

c ....

z ....

Listen again and write the words.

s ....

w ....

r ....

f ....

v ....

Listen, repeat, and copy.

① start

② watch

....

③ race

④ finish

....

⑤ video

....

Listen again and write the words.

p ....

m ....

c ....

b ....

s ....

Listen, repeat, and copy.

① purse

....

② money

....

③ cart

....

④ basket

....

⑤ shopping

....

Day 5

What can you remember from this week?

1. Look at the pictures and fill in the missing letters.

1 p _ a _ e

2 b _ t _ l _

3 g _ a _ s

4 b _ w _

5 c _ p

2. Read the words and check the correct pictures.

1 watch

A ☐   B ☐

2 finish

A ☐   B ☐

3 start

A ☐   B ☐

4 race

A ☐   B ☐

5 video

A ☐   B ☐

3. Look at the pictures and circle the correct words.

money

purse

shopping

basket

basket

cart

shopping

money

purse

cart

4. Look at the pictures and write the correct words.

z _ _ _

c _ _ _ _

m _ _ _ _ _ _

c _ _ _ _ _ _ _

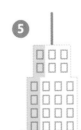

s _ _ _ _ _ _ _ _ _ _

Day 1

Listen, repeat, and copy.

① picnic

② path

③ blanket

④ bridge

⑤ stream

Listen again and write the words.

p ....

p ....

b ....

b ....

s ....

Day 2

Listen, repeat, and copy.

① tour

② view

③ photo

④ postcard

⑤ camera

Listen again and write the words.

t ....

v ....

p ....

p ....

c ....

Week 34

Listen again and write the words.

w ....

t ....

m ....

s ....

s ....

Listen, repeat, and copy.

① work

....

② travel

....

③ meet

....

④ speak

....

⑤ show

....

Listen again and write the words.

s ....

m ....

E ....

r ....

a ....

Listen, repeat, and copy.

① sun

....

② moon

....

③ Earth

....

④ rocket

....

⑤ astronaut

....

Day 5

What can you remember from this week?

1. Look at the pictures and write the letters in the correct order.

1. t l e a r v

t _ _ _ _ _

2. w r k o

w _ _ _

3. s a k p e

s _ _ _ _ _

4. m t e e

m _ _ _

5. s o h w

s _ _ _

2. Look at the pictures and check the correct words.

1. sun ☐
astronaut ☐
moon ☐

2. rocket ☐
Earth ☐
astronaut ☐

3. sun ☐
moon ☐
Earth ☐

4. moon ☐
rocket ☐
astronaut ☐

5. sun ☐
Earth ☐
rocket ☐

Week 34

3. Look at the pictures and write the correct words.

path	bridge	picnic	stream	blanket

1 b _ _ _ _ _ _

2 s _ _ _ _ _ _

3 p _ _ _ _

4 p _ _ _ _ _ _

5 b _ _ _ _ _ _ _

4. Look at the pictures and circle the correct words.

1 photo / camera

2 postcard / view

3 tour / camera

4 tour / view

5 photo / postcard

Day 1

Listen, repeat, and copy.

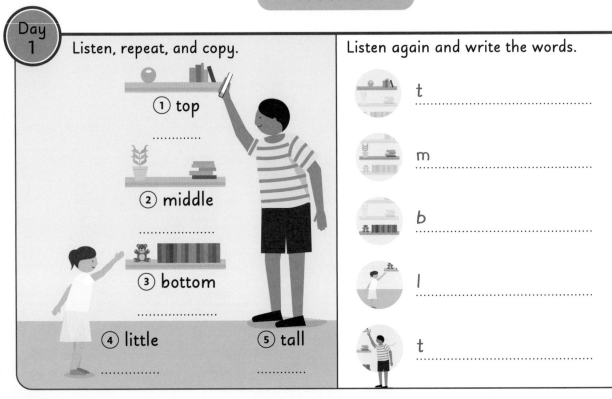

① top

② middle

③ bottom

④ little ⑤ tall

Listen again and write the words.

t ....

m ....

b ....

l ....

t ....

Day 2

Listen, repeat, and copy.

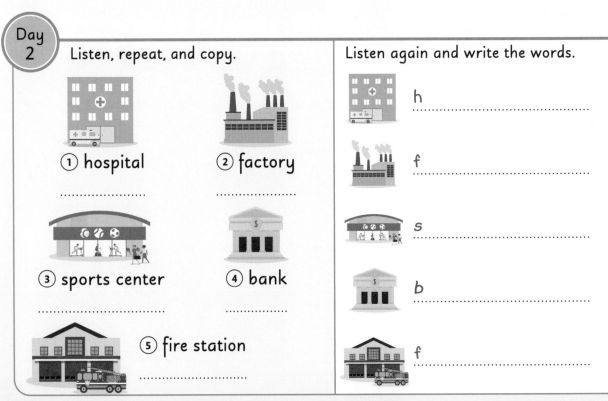

① hospital ② factory

③ sports center ④ bank

⑤ fire station

Listen again and write the words.

h ....

f ....

s ....

b ....

f ....

Week 35

Listen again and write the words.

w ....

d ....

w ....

h ....

c ....

Listen, repeat, and copy.

① wet   ② dry

....

③ warm

....

④ hot   ⑤ cold

....

Listen again and write the words.

b ....

w ....

s ....

s ....

r ....

Listen, repeat, and copy.

① borrow   ② whisper

....

③ search

....

④ study   ⑤ read

....

Week 35

Day 5 What can you remember from this week?

1. Read the words and check the correct pictures.

1 factory

A ☐ B ☐

2 sports center

A ☐ B ☐

3 bank

A ☐ B ☐

4 fire station

A ☐ B ☐

5 hospital

A ☐ B ☐

2. Look at the pictures and fill in the missing letters.

1    l _ t _ l _

2   b _ t _ o _

3   m _ d _ l _

4    t _ l _

5   t _ _ p

146

3. Look at the pictures and write the correct words.

w _ _ _

d _ _

w _ _

c _ _ _

h _ _

4. Match the pictures to the correct words.

   whisper

          study

   borrow

   search

          read

Week 36

Day 1

Listen, repeat, and copy.

① tea

② milk

③ sugar

④ coffee

⑤ cookie

Listen again and write the words.

t ....

m ....

s ....

c ....

c ....

Day 2

Listen, repeat, and copy.

① take off

② land

③ get off

④ get on

⑤ hurry

Listen again and write the words.

t ....

l ....

g ....

g ....

h ....

148

Listen again and write the words.

i ....

s ....

h ....

s ....

s ....

Listen, repeat, and copy.

① ice skates

....

② sled

....

③ hockey stick

....

④ skis

....

⑤ snowboard

....

Listen again and write the words.

g ....

s ....

b ....

r ....

w ....

Listen, repeat, and copy.

① gold

....

② silver

....

③ bronze

....

④ race

....

⑤ winner

....

2

1

3

Day 5

What can you remember from this week?

1. Look at the pictures and write the correct words.

> milk   tea   coffee
> sugar   cookie

 1 t _ _

 2 c _ _ _ _ _ _

 3 c _ _ _ _ _ _

 4 m _ _ _

 5 s _ _ _ _ _

2. Look at the pictures and circle the correct words.

 1 race / gold

 2 winner / silver

 3 silver / gold

 4 winner / bronze

 5 bronze / race

3. Look at the pictures and fill in the missing letters.

1 t _ k _ o _ f

2 _ a _ d

3 h _ _ r _ y

4 g _ t _ _ f _

5 _ e _ o _

4. Read the words and check the correct pictures.

1 skis

2 ice skates

3 sled

A ☐ B ☐   A ☐ B ☐   A ☐ B ☐

4 hockey stick

5 snowboard

A ☐ B ☐   A ☐ B ☐

Day 1

Listen, repeat, and copy.

① grass

....

② swan

....

③ duck

....

④ pond

....

⑤ frog

....

Listen again and write the words.

g ....

s ....

d ....

p ....

f ....

Day 2

Listen, repeat, and copy.

① prepare

....

② order

....

③ pay

....

④ like

....

⑤ don't like

....

Listen again and write the words.

p ....

o ....

p ....

l ....

d ....

Week 37

Listen again and write the words.

p ....

w ....

s ....

p ....

r ....

Listen, repeat, and copy.

① polar bear ....

② walrus ....

③ seal ....

④ penguin ....

⑤ reindeer ....

Listen again and write the words.

p ....

j ....

g ....

c ....

b ....

Listen, repeat, and copy.

① perfume ....

② jewelry ....

③ glasses ....

④ comb ....

⑤ brush ....

Day 5

What can you remember from this week?

1. Look at the pictures and write the correct words.

| pay | don't like | like | order | prepare |

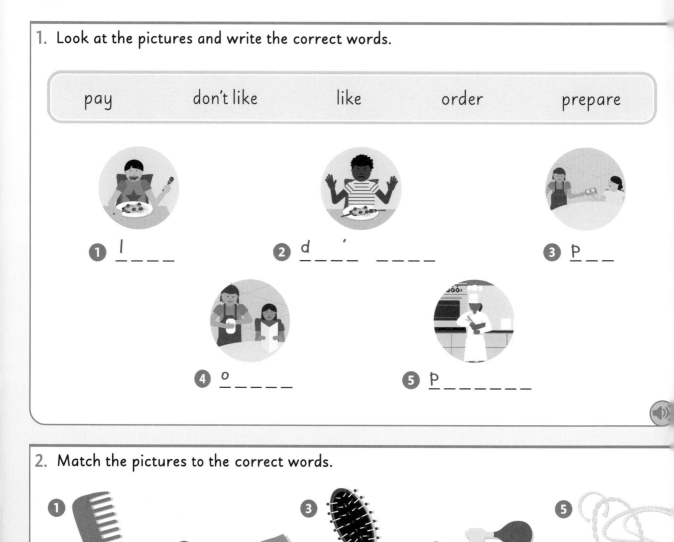

① l _ _ _ _

② d _ _ _ _ _ _ _ _

③ p _ _

④ o _ _ _ _ _

⑤ p _ _ _ _ _ _ _

2. Match the pictures to the correct words.

① ② ③ ④ ⑤

brush   comb   jewelry   glasses   perfume

Look at the pictures and check the correct words.

 1
penguin ☐
walrus ☐

 2
polar bear ☐
penguin ☐

 3
reindeer ☐
seal ☐

4
reindeer ☐
polar bear ☐

 5
seal ☐
walrus ☐

4. Look at the pictures and write the correct words.

 1
g _ _ _ _

 2
f _ _ _

 3
p _ _ _

 4
s _ _ _

 5
d _ _ _

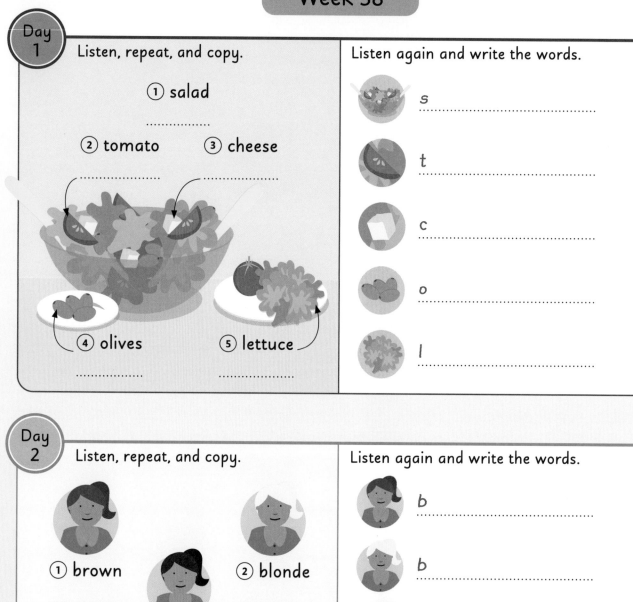

Day 1

Listen, repeat, and copy.

① salad

② tomato   ③ cheese

④ olives   ⑤ lettuce

Listen again and write the words.

s ....

t ....

c ....

o ....

l ....

Day 2

Listen, repeat, and copy.

① brown   ③ black   ② blonde

④ gray   ⑤ red

Listen again and write the words.

b ....

b ....

b ....

g ....

r ....

Week 38

Day 3

Listen again and write the words.

a ....

g ....

b ....

v ....

g ....

Listen, repeat, and copy.

① arrive
....

② greet
....

③ bring
....

④ visit
....

⑤ give
....

Day 4

Listen again and write the words.

a ....

a ....

p ....

v ....

s ....

Listen, repeat, and copy.

① airport
....

② airplane
....

③ pilot
....

④ vacation
....

⑤ suitcase
....

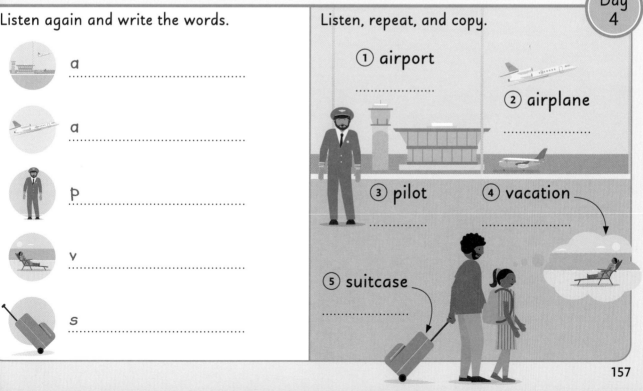

Day
5

What can you remember from this week?

1. Look at the pictures and check the correct words.

   1. airplane ☐
      pilot ☐
      vacation ☐

   2. suitcase ☐
      airplane ☐
      airport ☐

   3. vacation ☐
      suitcase ☐
      pilot ☐

   4. vacation ☐
      suitcase ☐
      airport ☐

   5. pilot ☐
      airport ☐
      airplane ☐

2. Look at the pictures and write the letters in the correct order.

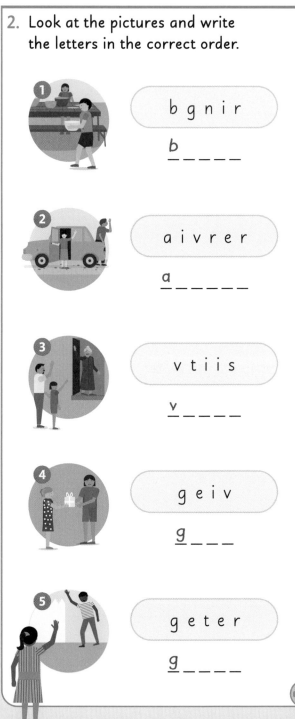

   1. b g n i r
      b _ _ _ _ _

   2. a i v r e r
      a _ _ _ _ _

   3. v t i i s
      v _ _ _ _

   4. g e i v
      g _ _ _

   5. g e t e r
      g _ _ _ _

3. Look at the pictures and write the correct words.

| gray | blonde | black | red | brown |

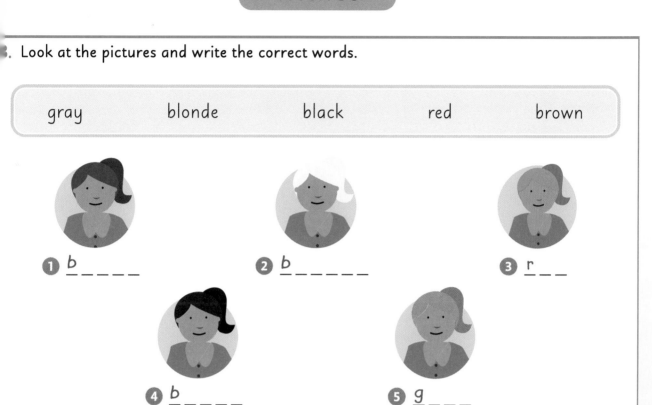

1 b _ _ _ _ _

2 b _ _ _ _ _ _

3 r _ _ _

4 b _ _ _ _ _

5 g _ _ _ _

4. Look at the picture and write the correct words.

olives

cheese

salad

tomato

lettuce

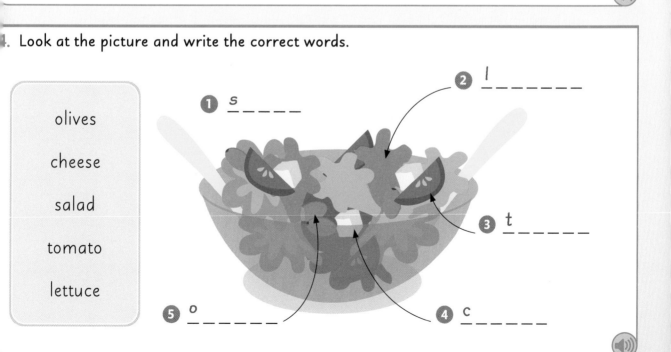

1 s _ _ _ _ _

2 l _ _ _ _ _ _ _

3 t _ _ _ _ _ _

4 c _ _ _ _ _ _

5 o _ _ _ _ _ _

Day 1

Listen, repeat, and copy.

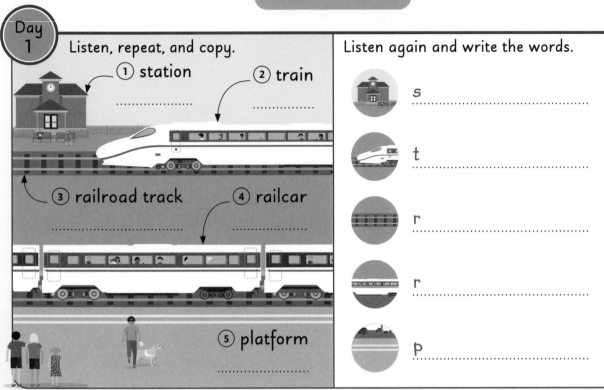

① station

② train

③ railroad track

④ railcar

⑤ platform

Listen again and write the words.

s.................................

t.................................

r.................................

r.................................

p.................................

Day 2

Listen, repeat, and copy.

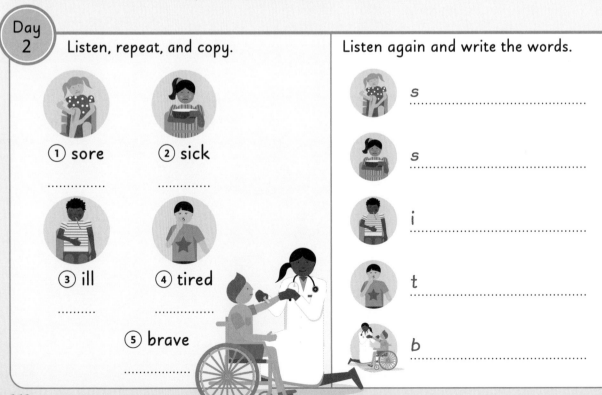

① sore

② sick

③ ill

④ tired

⑤ brave

Listen again and write the words.

s.................................

s.................................

i.................................

t.................................

b.................................

160

Day 3

Listen again and write the words.

m ......

s ......

k ......

p ......

t ......

Listen, repeat, and copy.

① match

② score
......

③ kick
......

④ player
......

⑤ team
......

Day 4

Listen again and write the words.

b ......

f ......

s ......

b ......

s ......

Listen, repeat, and copy.

① butterfly
......

② fly
......

③ spider
......

④ beetle
......

⑤ snail
......

161

Day
5

What can you remember from this week?

1. Look at the pictures and circle the correct words.

 match / team

 kick / score

 kick / team

 player / score

 player / match

2. Look at the pictures and fill in the missing letters.

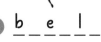

❶ b _ e _ l _

❷ _ l _

❸ b _ t _ e _ f _ y

❹ s _ a _ l _

❺ s _ i _ e _

3. Look at the pictures and write the letters in the correct order.

1 b e r a v

b _ _ _ _

2 s k i c

s _ _ _

3 s r e o

s _ _ _

4 t r i d e

t _ _ _ _

5 l i l

i _ _

4. Read the words and check the correct pictures.

1 train   A ☐   B ☐

2 station   A ☐   B ☐

3 platform   A ☐   B ☐

4 railroad
  track   A ☐   B ☐

5 railcar   A ☐   B ☐

Day 1

Listen, repeat, and copy.

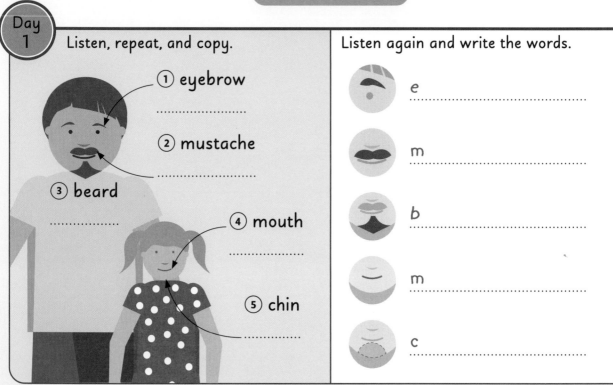

① eyebrow

② mustache

③ beard

④ mouth

⑤ chin

Listen again and write the words.

e ....

m ....

b ....

m ....

c ....

Day 2

Listen, repeat, and copy.

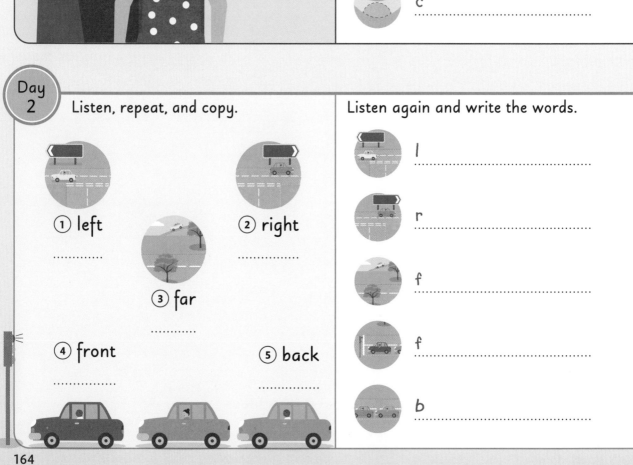

① left

② right

③ far

④ front

⑤ back

Listen again and write the words.

l ....

r ....

f ....

f ....

b ....

Listen again and write the words.

b ....

f ....

h ....

f ....

l ....

Listen, repeat, and copy.

① break

② fetch

....

....

③ hide

④ feed

....

....

⑤ look after

....

Listen again and write the words.

l ....

d ....

a ....

a ....

l ....

Listen, repeat, and copy.

① light

② dark

....

....

③ awake

④ asleep

....

....

⑤ loud

....

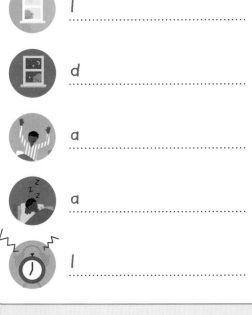

Day 5

What can you remember from this week?

1. Look at the pictures and write the letters in the correct order.

l t h i g

l _ _ _ _ _

a k e w a

a _ _ _ _ _

d k r a

d _ _ _ _

a p e l e s

a _ _ _ _ _ _

l d u o

l _ _ _ _

2. Match the pictures to the correct words.

fetch   hide   look after   feed   break

3. Look at the pictures and check the correct words.

1
far ☐
right ☐

2
back ☐
left ☐

3
far ☐
back ☐

4
front ☐
right ☐

5
front ☐
left ☐

4. Look at the pictures and write the correct words.

eyebrow   mouth   chin
mustache   beard

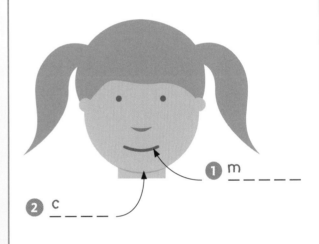
1 m _ _ _ _ _

2 c _ _ _ _

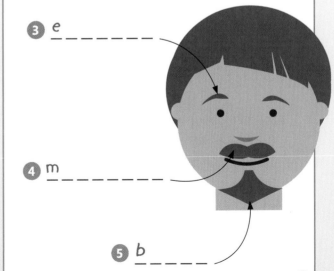
3 e _ _ _ _ _ _

4 m _ _ _ _ _ _ _ _

5 b _ _ _ _

Day 1

Listen, repeat, and copy.

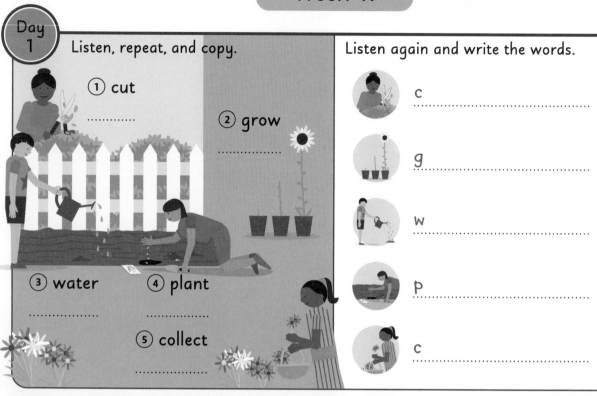

① cut

② grow

③ water   ④ plant

⑤ collect

Listen again and write the words.

c ....

g..................................

w ....

p..................................

c..................................

Day 2

Listen, repeat, and copy.

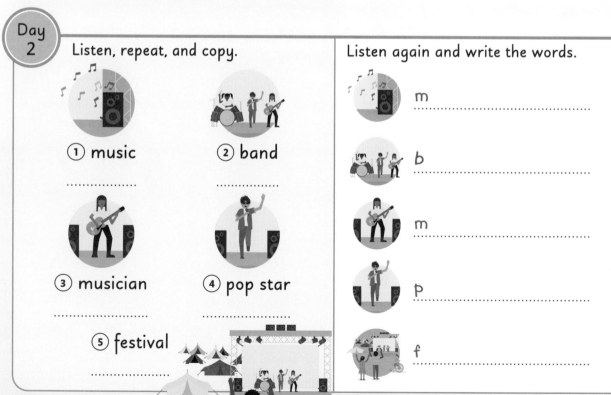

① music   ② band

③ musician   ④ pop star

⑤ festival

Listen again and write the words.

m..................................

b..................................

m..................................

p..................................

f..................................

Listen again and write the words.

h ....

q ....

w ....

c ....

c ....

Listen, repeat, and copy.

① half
....

② quarter
....

③ whole
....

④ corner
....

⑤ center
....

Listen again and write the words.

h ....

l ....

s ....

p ....

h ....

Listen, repeat, and copy.

① hotel
....

② lounge chair
....

③ sunglasses
....

④ pool
....

⑤ hat
....

Day 5

What can you remember from this week?

---

1. Look at the pictures and write the correct words.

center   whole   half
corner   quarter

  1. w _ _ _ _

 2. c _ _ _ _ _

 3. h _ _ _

  4. c _ _ _ _ _

 5. q _ _ _ _ _ _

---

2. Look at the pictures and circle the correct words.

  1. sunglasses
   pool

 2. hat
   lounge chair

  3. hotel
   pool

 4. lounge chair
   hotel

 5. hat
   sunglasses

Week 41

3. Read the words and check the correct pictures.

1 festival

A ☐   B ☐

2 musician

A ☐   B ☐

3 music

A ☐   B ☐

4 pop star
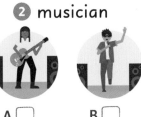
A ☐   B ☐

5 band
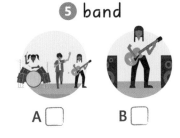
A ☐   B ☐

4. Look at the pictures and write the correct words.

1 c _ _ _ _ _ _ _

2 p _ _ _ _ _

3 w _ _ _ _ _

4 g _ _ _ _

5 c _ _ _

171

Day 1

Listen, repeat, and copy.

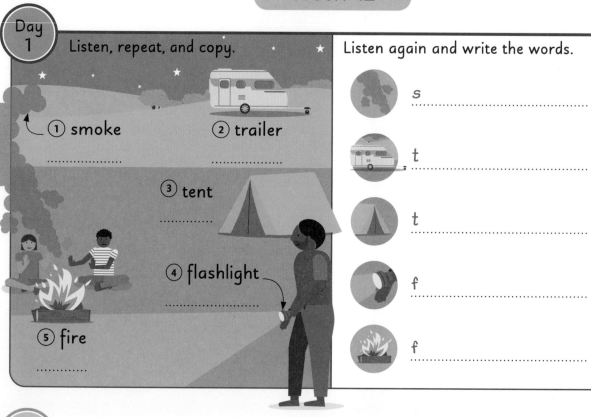

① smoke

② trailer

③ tent

④ flashlight

⑤ fire

Listen again and write the words.

s ....

t ....

t ....

f ....

f ....

Day 2

Listen, repeat, and copy.

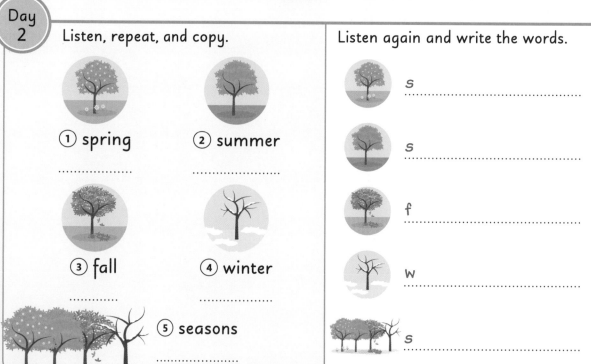

① spring

② summer

③ fall

④ winter

⑤ seasons

Listen again and write the words.

s ....

s ....

f ....

w ....

s ....

Listen again and write the words.

`12:01` c ....

`12:00` h ....

`12:01` m ....

m ....

m ....

Listen, repeat, and copy.

① clock
....

`12:01`

② hour ....   ③ minute ....

④ midday ....   ⑤ midnight ....

Listen again and write the words.

e ....

m ....

t ....

g ....

t ....

Listen, repeat, and copy.

① engineer ....

② machine ....

③ toolbox ....   ④ glue ....

⑤ tools ....

Day 5

What can you remember from this week?

---

1. Look at the pictures and fill in the missing letters.

1 _c_ _o_ _k_

2 _ _i_ _d_ _y_

3 _m_ _n_ _t_ _

4 _m_ _d_ _i_ _h_ _ _

5 _h_ _u_ _

---

2. Look at the pictures and circle the correct words.

1 fire / tent

2 smoke / trailer

3 tent / flashlight

4 trailer / flashlight

5 smoke / fire

3. Look at the pictures and write the correct words.

1 s _ _ _ _ _ _

2 w _ _ _ _ _ _

3 f _ _ _ _

4 s _ _ _ _ _ _

5

s _ _ _ _ _ _

4. Look at the pictures and check the correct words.

1 glue ☐
    machine ☐

2 tools ☐
    engineer ☐

3 toolbox ☐
    glue ☐

4 engineer ☐
    tools ☐

5 machine ☐
    toolbox ☐

Day 1

Listen, repeat, and copy.

① carry ② weigh ③ sell

....

④ buy ⑤ give

....

Listen again and write the words.

c ....

w ....

s ....

b ....

g ....

Day 2

Listen, repeat, and copy.

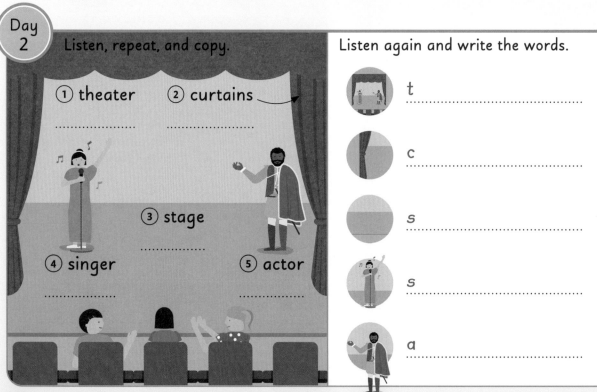

① theater ② curtains

....

③ stage

....

④ singer ⑤ actor

....

Listen again and write the words.

t ....

c ....

s ....

s ....

a ....

Listen again and write the words.

f ....

b ....

s ....

s ....

b ....

Listen, repeat, and copy.

① flag
....

② beach ball
....

③ shovel
....

④ sandcastle
....

⑤ bucket
....

Listen again and write the words.

w ....

w ....

m ....

y ....

d ....

Listen, repeat, and copy.

① week
....

② weekend
....

③ month
....

④ year
....

⑤ diary
....

Week 43

Day 5

What can you remember from this week?

1. Look at the pictures and write the letters in the correct order.

w g i e h

w _ _ _ _ _

b y u

b _ _ _

g e i v

g _ _ _ _

s l e l

s _ _ _ _

c y r a r

c _ _ _ _ _

2. Look at the pictures and circle the correct words.

theater

actor

curtains

singer

actor

stage

singer

stage

curtains

theater

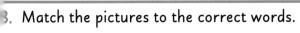
3. Match the pictures to the correct words.

1 **2** **3** **4** **5**

bucket   flag   sandcastle   beach ball   shovel

4. Look at the pictures and write the correct words.

| week | month | weekend | year | diary |

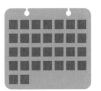

1 m _ _ _ _

2 w _ _ _ _

3 y _ _ _

4 d _ _ _ _ _

5 w _ _ _ _ _ _ _

Day 1

Listen, repeat, and copy.

① flour

② jam

③ honey

④ chocolate

⑤ butter

Listen again and write the words.

f ....

j ....

h ....

c ....

b ....

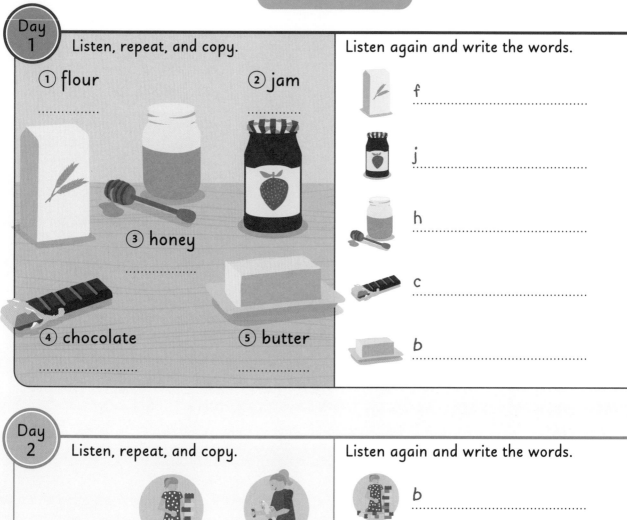

Day 2

Listen, repeat, and copy.

① build

② fix

③ mix

④ glue

⑤ paint

Listen again and write the words.

b ....

f ....

m ....

g ....

p ....

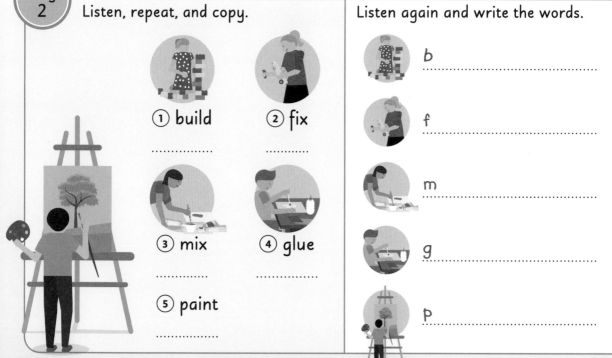

Listen again and write the words.

 t ....

 E ....

 m ....

 a ....

 s ....

Listen, repeat, and copy.

① timetable

② English

....

....

③ math

④ art

....

....

⑤ science

....

Listen again and write the words.

 s ....

 f ....

 t ....

 f ....

 f ....

Listen, repeat, and copy.

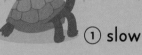

① slow

② fast

....

....

③ thin

④ fat

⑤ furry

....

....

....

Day 5

What can you remember from this week?

---

1. Look at the pictures and circle the correct words.

 **①** English / art

 **②** math / science

 **③** timetable / science

 **④** English / math

 **⑤** art / timetable

---

2. Look at the pictures and fill in the missing letters.

 **①** b _ i _ d

 **②** p _ i _ t

 **③** _ _ i _

 **④** f _ _ x

⑤ _ _ l _ e

3. Look at the pictures and check the correct words.

1. jam ☐
   butter ☐
   chocolate ☐

2. flour ☐
   honey ☐
   jam ☐

3. butter ☐
   chocolate ☐
   honey ☐

4. flour ☐
   butter ☐
   jam ☐

5. honey ☐
   chocolate ☐
   flour ☐

4. Look at the pictures and write the correct words.

slow   furry   fast
     fat   thin

1. f _ _ _ _

2. s _ _ _

3. f _ _

4. f _ _ _

5. t _ _ _

Week 45

Day 1

Listen, repeat, and copy.

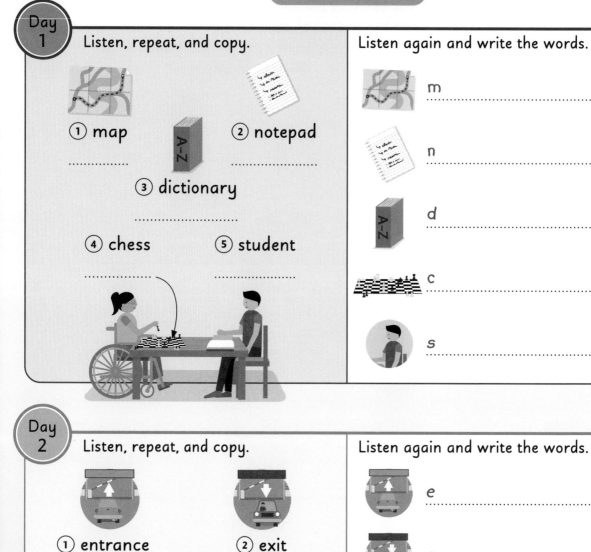

① map

② notepad

③ dictionary

④ chess

⑤ student

Listen again and write the words.

m ....

n ....

d ....

c ....

s ....

Day 2

Listen, repeat, and copy.

① entrance

② exit

③ parking lot

④ stores

⑤ shopping center

Listen again and write the words.

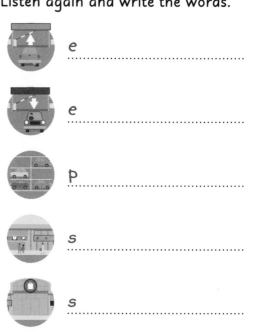

e ....

e ....

p ....

s ....

s ....

184

Listen again and write the words.

m ....

b ....

X- ....

b ....

m ....

Listen, repeat, and copy.

① mask

....

② bandage

....

③ X-ray

....

④ band-aid

....

⑤ medicine

....

Listen again and write the words.

c ....

l ....

c ....

b ....

s ....

Listen, repeat, and copy.

① camp

....

② laugh

....

③ chat

....

④ burn

....

⑤ sleep

....

Day 5

What can you remember from this week?

1. Look at the pictures and circle the correct words.

entrance

exit

parking lot

shopping center

stores

parking lot

entrance

stores

exit

shopping center

2. Look at the pictures and write the correct words.

s _ _ _ _ _ _ _

m _ _ _

c _ _ _ _ _

d _ _ _ _ _ _ _ _ _

n _ _ _ _ _ _

3. Look at the pictures and check the correct words.

1
medicine ☐
mask ☐

2
band-aid ☐
X-ray ☐

3
X-ray ☐
bandage ☐

4
medicine ☐
band-aid ☐

5
mask ☐
bandage ☐

4. Look at the pictures and fill in the missing letters.

1 b _ r _

2 l _ u _ h

3 _ c _ a _

4 c _ m _

5 s _ e _ p

Day 1

Listen, repeat, and copy.

Listen again and write the words.

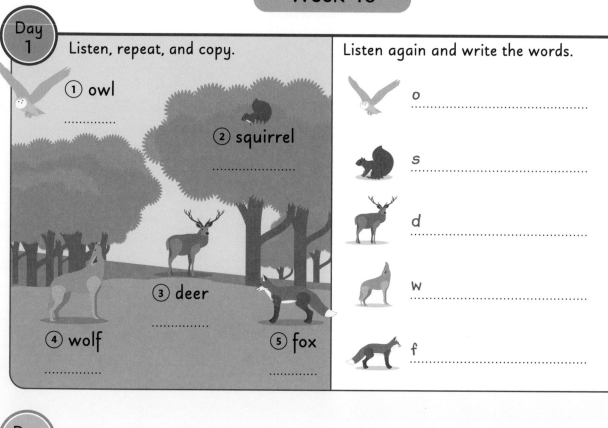

① owl
....

② squirrel
....

③ deer
....

④ wolf
....

⑤ fox
....

o ....

s ....

d ....

w ....

f ....

Day 2

Listen, repeat, and copy.

Listen again and write the words.

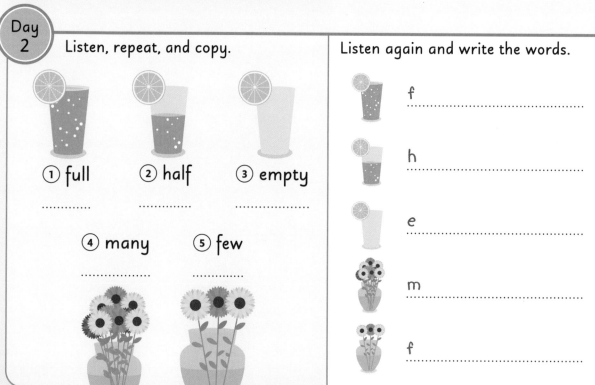

① full
....

② half
....

③ empty
....

④ many
....

⑤ few
....

f ....

h ....

e ....

m ....

f ....

Listen again and write the words.

c ....

s ....

s ....

r ....

s ....

Listen, repeat, and copy.

① crab

....

② seaweed

....

③ starfish

....

④ rocks

....

⑤ shell

....

Listen again and write the words.

n ....

m ....

c ....

p ....

c ....

Listen, repeat, and copy.

① newspaper

....

② magazine

....

③ comic book

....

④ puzzle book

....

⑤ cartoon

....

Day 5

What can you remember from this week?

1. Look at the pictures and write the correct words.

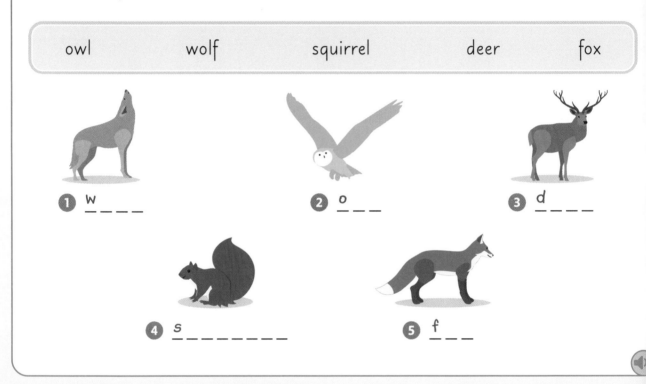

owl   wolf   squirrel   deer   fox

1 w _ _ _ _

2 o _ _ _

3 d _ _ _ _

4 s _ _ _ _ _ _ _ _

5 f _ _ _

2. Match the pictures to the correct words.

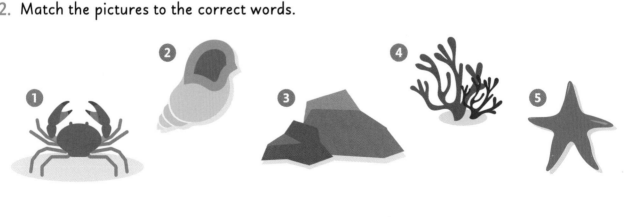

shell   crab   starfish   rocks   seaweed

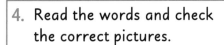

Week 46

3. Look at the pictures and write the correct words.

1 f _ _ _

2 e _ _ _ _

3 h _ _ _

4 f _ _

5 m _ _ _

4. Read the words and check the correct pictures.

1 magazine   A ☐   B ☐

2 puzzle book   A ☐   B ☐

3 newspaper   A ☐   B ☐

4 comic book   A ☐   B ☐

5 cartoon   A ☐   B ☐

Day 1

Listen, repeat, and copy.

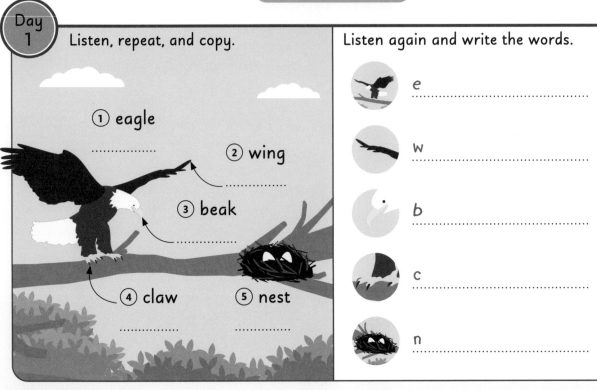

① eagle

② wing

③ beak

④ claw

⑤ nest

Listen again and write the words.

e ....

w ....

b ....

c ....

n ....

Day 2

Listen, repeat, and copy.

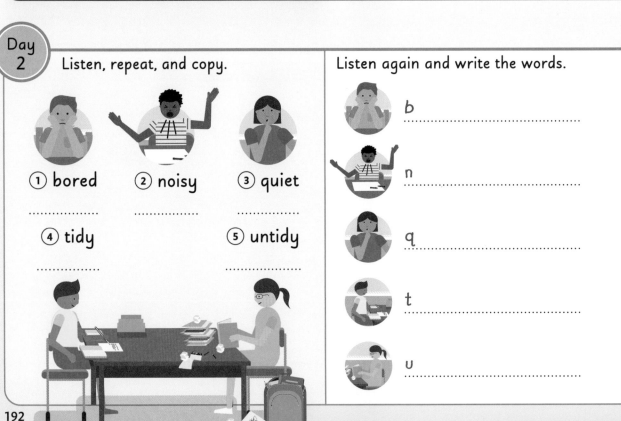

① bored

② noisy

③ quiet

④ tidy

⑤ untidy

Listen again and write the words.

b ....

n ....

q ....

t ....

u ....

192

Day 3

Listen again and write the words.

s ....

s ....

i ....

i ....

s ....

Listen, repeat, and copy.

① skiing   ② sledding

....

③ ice hockey   ④ ice-skating

....

⑤ snowboarding

....

Day 4

Listen again and write the words.

h ....

g ....

d ....

l ....

s ....

Listen, repeat, and copy.

① history   ② geography

....

③ design   ④ languages

....

⑤ subjects

....

Day 5

What can you remember from this week?

1. Look at the pictures and check the correct words.

 ❶
geography ☐
subjects ☐

❷
languages ☐
design ☐

❸
history ☐
geography ☐

❹
languages ☐
history ☐

❺
design ☐
subjects ☐

2. Look at the pictures and fill in the missing letters.

❶
n _ s _

❷
_ e _ k

❸
w _ n _

❹
_ l _ w

❺
e _ g _ e

3. Look at the pictures and write the correct words.

① n _ _ _ _
② q _ _ _ _ _
③ u _ _ _ _ _ _

④ t _ _ _ _
⑤ b _ _ _ _ _

4. Read the words and check the correct pictures.

① sledding
② snowboarding
③ skiing

A ☐   B ☐

A ☐   B ☐

A ☐   B ☐

④ ice-skating
⑤ ice hockey

A ☐   B ☐

A ☐   B ☐

Week 48

Day 1

Listen, repeat, and copy.

Listen again and write the words.

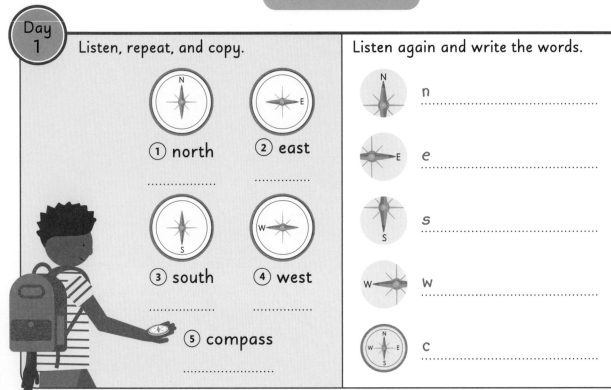

① north

② east

③ south

④ west

⑤ compass

n ....

e ....

s ....

w ....

c ....

Day 2

Listen, repeat, and copy.

Listen again and write the words.

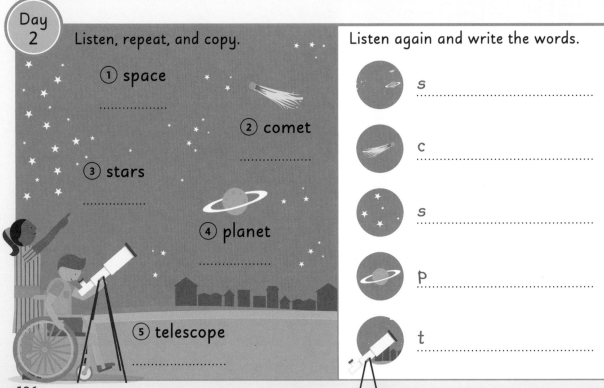

① space

② comet

③ stars

④ planet

⑤ telescope

s ....

c ....

s ....

p ....

t ....

Listen again and write the words.

n ....

p ....

r ....

b ....

w ....

Listen, repeat, and copy.

① necklace   ② purse

....

③ ring

....

④ bracelet   ⑤ watch

....

Listen again and write the words.

j ....

d ....

a ....

p ....

j ....

Listen, repeat, and copy.

① journalist   ② designer

....

③ artist   ④ photographer

....

⑤ jobs

....

Day 5   What can you remember from this week?

1. Look at the picture and write the correct words.

west

north

compass

south

east

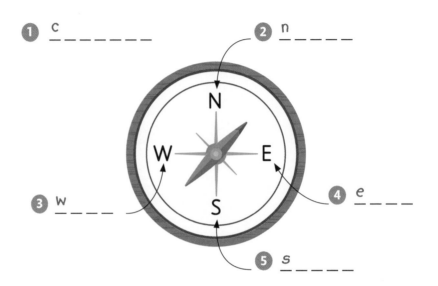

1 c _ _ _ _ _ _ _

2 n _ _ _ _ _

3 w _ _ _ _

4 e _ _ _ _

5 s _ _ _ _ _

2. Look at the pictures and circle the correct words.

1  jobs

artist

2  photographer

designer

3  journalist

designer

4  artist

journalist

5  jobs

photographer

3. Match the pictures to the correct words.

 **1**　　　purse

 **2**　　　ring

 **3**　　　bracelet

 **4**　　　watch

 **5**　　　necklace

4. Look at the pictures and write the correct words.

> stars　　comet　　planet
> space　　telescope

 **1**　　c _ _ _ _

 **2**　　s _ _ _ _

 **3**　　p _ _ _ _ _

 4　　s _ _ _ _

 **5**　　t _ _ _ _ _ _ _ _

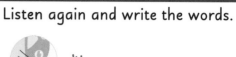

Week 49

Day 1

Listen, repeat, and copy.

① whiskers

....

② collar

....

③ fur

....

④ paw

....

⑤ tail

....

Listen again and write the words.

 w ....

 c ....

 f ....

 p ....

 t ....

Day 2

Listen, repeat, and copy.

① invent
....

③ think
....

④ act
....

② design
....

⑤ explore
....

Listen again and write the words.

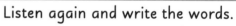

 i ....

 d ....

 t ....

 a ....

 e ....

200

Week 49

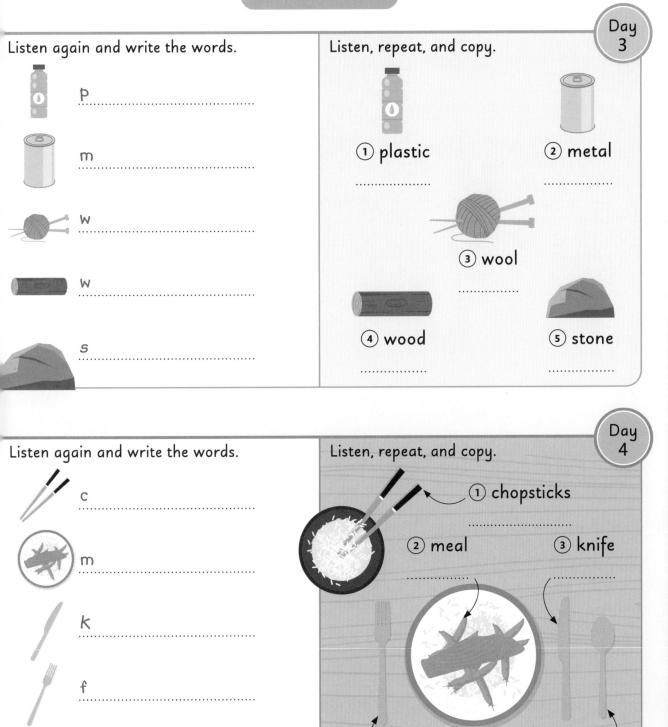

Listen again and write the words.

p.....................................

m.....................................

w.....................................

w.....................................

s.....................................

Listen, repeat, and copy.

① plastic   ② metal

....

③ wool

....

④ wood   ⑤ stone

....

Listen again and write the words.

c.....................................

m.....................................

k.....................................

f.....................................

s.....................................

Listen, repeat, and copy.

① chopsticks

....

② meal   ③ knife

....

④ fork   ⑤ spoon

....

Day
5

What can you remember from this week?

1. Read the words and check the correct pictures.

❶ fork

A ☐   B ☐

❷ meal

A ☐   B ☐

❸ knife

A ☐   B ☐

❹ chopsticks

A ☐   B ☐

❺ spoon

A ☐   B ☐

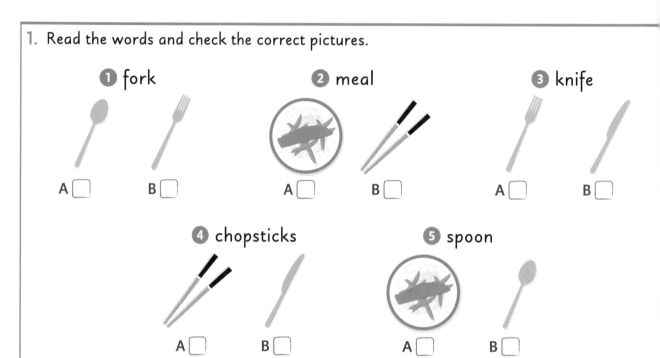

2. Look at the pictures and fill in the missing letters.

❶ m _ t _ l

❷ _ t _ n _

❸ _ o _ d

❹ p _ a _ t _ c

❺ w _ o _

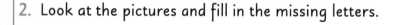
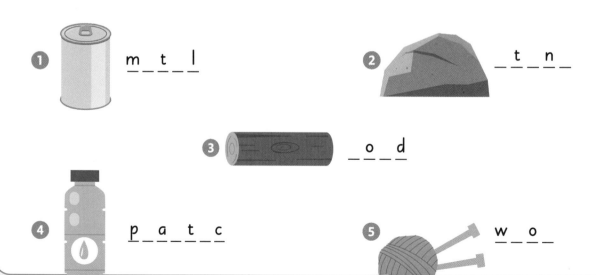

3. Look at the pictures and check the correct words.

1. collar ☐
   whiskers ☐
   fur ☐

2. collar ☐
   tail ☐
   paw ☐

3. tail ☐
   fur ☐
   whiskers ☐

4. whiskers ☐
   collar ☐
   paw ☐

5. fur ☐
   paw ☐
   tail ☐

4. Look at the pictures and write the letters in the correct order.

1. i t n v e n
   i _ _ _ _ _ _

2. t k n i h
   t _ _ _ _ _

3. e l o p r e x
   e _ _ _ _ _ _

4. a t c
   a _ _

5. d g n s i e
   d _ _ _ _ _

Day 1

Listen, repeat, and copy.

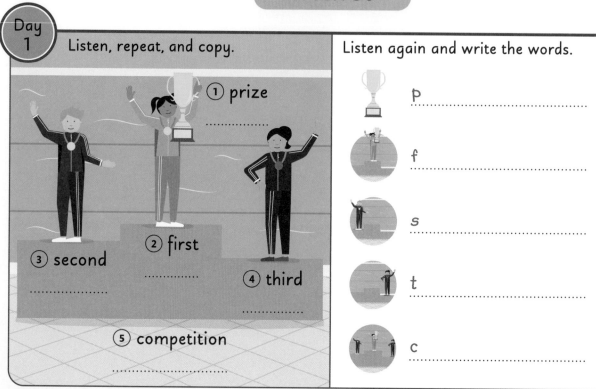

① prize

② first

③ second

④ third

⑤ competition

Listen again and write the words.

p ....

f ....

s ....

t ....

c ....

Day 2

Listen, repeat, and copy.

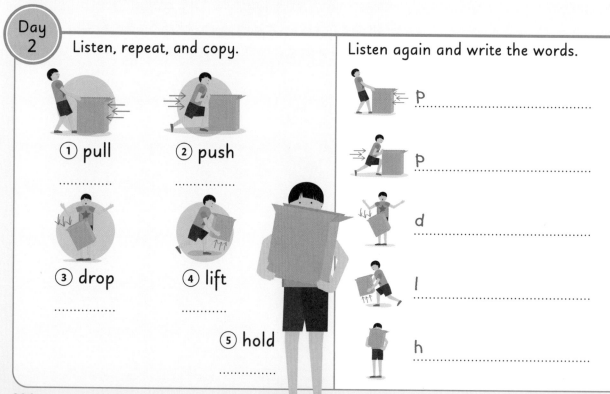

① pull

② push

③ drop

④ lift

⑤ hold

Listen again and write the words.

p ....

p ....

d ....

l ....

h ....

Listen again and write the words.

p ....

h ....

r ....

m ....

c ....

Listen, repeat, and copy.

① plumber ....

② hairdresser ....

③ receptionist ....

④ mail carrier ....

⑤ cleaner ....

Listen again and write the words.

s ....

p ....

p ....

c ....

e ....

Listen, repeat, and copy.

① stripes ....

② pattern ....

③ polka dots ....

④ cheap ....

⑤ expensive ....

What can you remember from this week?

1. Look at the pictures and circle the correct words.

 ①   push / pull

 ②   hold / drop

①   ③    lift / push

④    drop / pull

⑤    hold / lift

2. Look at the pictures and write the correct words.

 ①   s _ _ _ _ _ _

② 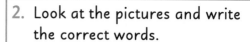   e _ _ _ _ _ _ _ _

③    p _ _ _ _ _ _ _ _

④    p _ _ _ _ _ _

⑤    c _ _ _ _ _

3. Look at the pictures and write the correct words.

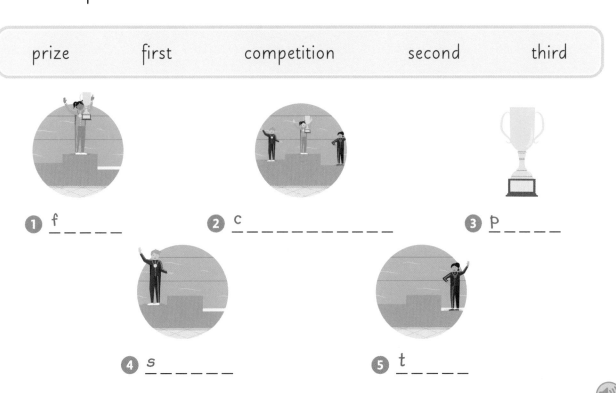

| prize | first | competition | second | third |

1 f _ _ _ _ _

2 c _ _ _ _ _ _ _ _ _ _ _

3 P _ _ _ _ _

4 s _ _ _ _ _ _

5 t _ _ _ _ _

4. Match the pictures to the correct words.

hairdresser   mail carrier   cleaner   receptionist   plumber

Day 1

Listen, repeat, and copy.

① queen   ② king

③ princess   ④ prince

⑤ crown

Listen again and write the words.

q ....

k ....

p ....

p ....

c ....

Day 2

Listen, repeat, and copy.

① soft   ② hard

③ strong   ④ weak

⑤ broken

Listen again and write the words.

s ....

h ....

s ....

w ....

b ....

Listen again and write the words.

l ....

r ....

t ....

t ....

c ....

Listen, repeat, and copy.

① look for ....

② repair ....

③ turn on ....

④ turn off ....

⑤ change ....

Listen again and write the words.

t ....

z ....

b ....

p ....

b ....

Listen, repeat, and copy.

① tie ....

② zipper ....

③ button ....

④ pocket ....

⑤ belt ....

Week 51

Day 5

What can you remember from this week?

1. Look at the pictures and fill in the missing letters.

① c _ a _ g _

② _ o _ k _ _ o _

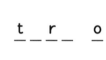

③ t _ r _ o _

④ _ u _ n _ _ f _

⑤ r _ p _ i _

2. Look at the pictures and circle the correct words.

① tie / button

② pocket / button

③ belt / zipper

④ pocket / zipper

⑤ tie / belt

210

3. Look at the pictures and write the letters in the correct order.

1. s t o g n r

    s _ _ _ _ _

2. s f o t

    s _ _ _

3. h r a d

    h _ _ _

4. b k n e o r

    b _ _ _ _ _

5. w k a e

    w _ _ _

4. Look at the pictures and check the correct words.

1. princess ☐
    crown ☐

2. queen ☐
    king ☐

3. princess ☐
    prince ☐

4. crown ☐
    king ☐

5. queen ☐
    prince ☐

Week 52

Day 1

Listen, repeat, and copy.

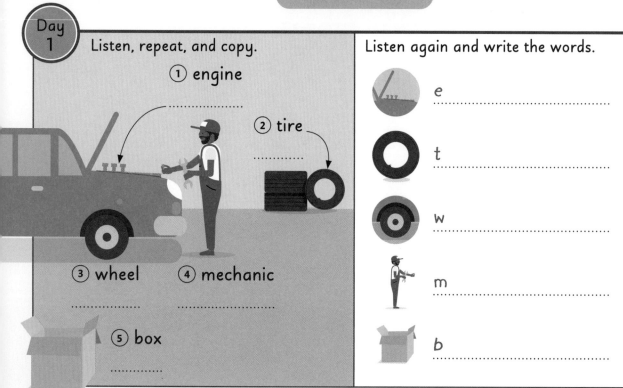

① engine

② tire

③ wheel   ④ mechanic

⑤ box

Listen again and write the words.

e ....

t ....

w ....

m ....

b ....

Day 2

Listen, repeat, and copy.

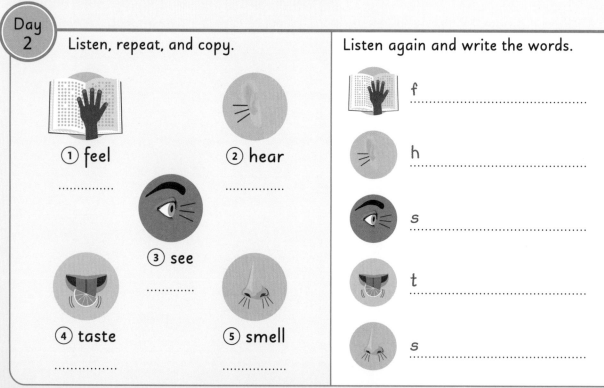

① feel   ② hear

③ see

④ taste   ⑤ smell

Listen again and write the words.

f ....

h ....

s ....

t ....

s ....

Week 52

Listen again and write the words.

v ....

d ....

i ....

c ....

m ....

Listen, repeat, and copy.

① violin
....

② drum
....

③ instruments
....

④ concert
....

⑤ music
....

Listen again and write the words.

p ....

p ....

m ....

p ....

s ....

Listen, repeat, and copy.

① pot
....

② pan
....

③ microwave
....

④ pepper
....

⑤ salt
....

Day 5

What can you remember from this week?

1. Look at the pictures and write the correct words.

 ① p _ _ _ _ _ _

 ② s _ _ _ _

 ③ m _ _ _ _ _ _ _ _ _

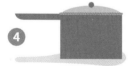 ④ p _ _ _

 ⑤ p _ _

2. Match the pictures to the correct words.

 ①   music

 ②   drum

 ③   violin

 ④   concert

 ⑤   instruments

3. Look at the pictures and write the correct words.

| feel | taste | hear | smell | see |

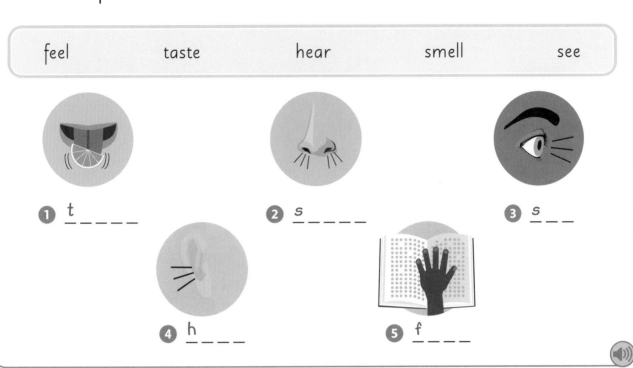

❶ t _ _ _ _

❷ s _ _ _ _

❸ s _ _

❹ h _ _ _

❺ f _ _ _

4. Read the words and check the correct pictures.

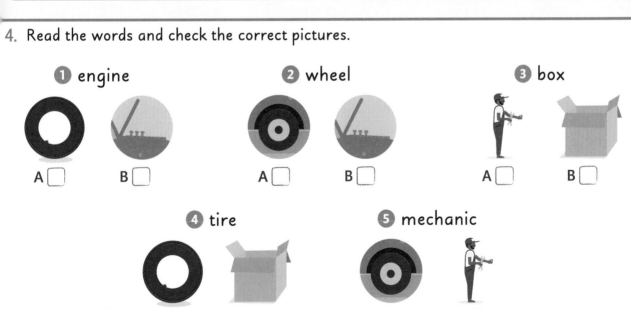

❶ engine

A ☐   B ☐

❷ wheel

A ☐   B ☐

❸ box

A ☐   B ☐

❹ tire

A ☐   B ☐

❺ mechanic

A ☐   B ☐

Numbers

Listen, repeat, and copy.

0 ① zero **10** ② ten **20** ③ twenty **30** ④ thirty **40** ⑤ forty **50** ⑥ fifty

60 ⑦ sixty **70** ⑧ seventy **80** ⑨ eighty **90** ⑩ ninety

91 ⑪ ninety-one **92** ⑫ ninety-two **93** ⑬ ninety-three

94 ⑭ ninety-four **95** ⑮ ninety-five **96** ⑯ ninety-six

97 ⑰ ninety-seven **98** ⑱ ninety-eight **99** ⑲ ninety-nine

100 ⑳ one hundred **1 000** ㉑ one thousand **1 000 000** ㉒ one million

Days

Listen, repeat, and copy.

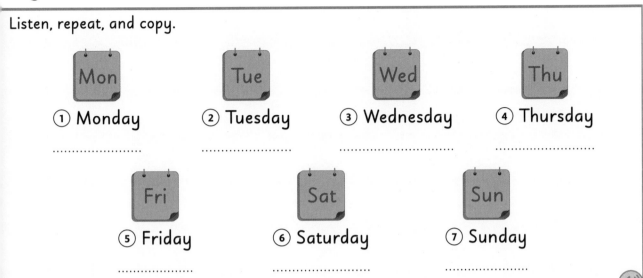

1 Monday 2 Tuesday 3 Wednesday 4 Thursday

5 Friday 6 Saturday 7 Sunday

Months

Listen, repeat, and copy

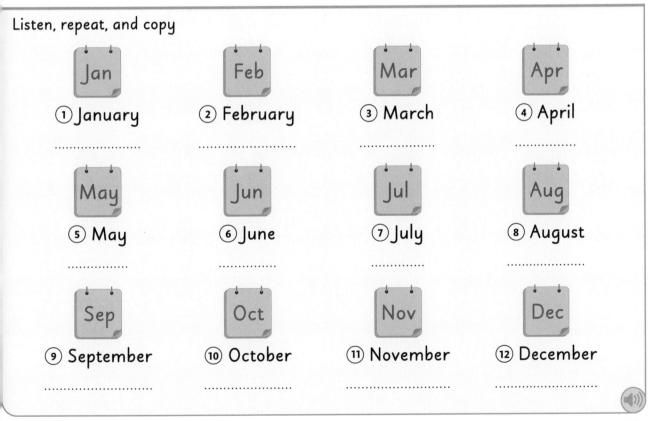

1 January 2 February 3 March 4 April

5 May 6 June 7 July 8 August

9 September 10 October 11 November 12 December

Word list

Each word is followed by the number of the week it appears in. For words that are not in a weekly unit, a page number is given (for example, **p216**).

KEY

adj	adjective
n	noun
num	number
prep	preposition
v	verb

A

act *v* **49**
action figure *n* **2**
actor *n* **43**
add *v* **10**
address *n* **30**
afraid *adj* **12**
afternoon *n* **8**
airplane *n* **38**
airport *n* **38**
alphabet *n* **2**
ambulance *n* **25**
angry *adj* **12**
animals *n* **10**
answer *v* **5**
ant *n* **17**
apartment *n* **12**
apartment building *n* **12**
apple *n* **1**
apps *n* **21**
April *n* **p217**
arm *n* **6**
armchair *n* **7**
arrive *v* **38**
art *n* **44**
artist *n* **48**
ask *v* **17**
asleep *adj* **40**
astronaut *n* **34**
August *n* **p217**
aunt *n* **14**
awake *adj* **40**

B

baby *n* **7**
back *adj* **40**
back *n* **23**
backpack *n* **5**
badminton *n* **6**
balcony *n* **12**
ball *n* **6**
balloon *n* **16**
banana *n* **1**
band *n* **41**
bandage *n* **45**
band-aid *n* **45**
bank *n* **35**
barn *n* **10**
baseball *n* **6**
baseball cap *n* **11**
basement *n* **22**
basket *n* **33**
basketball *n* **6**
bat *n* **15**
bathroom *n* **4**
bathtub *n* **26**
beach *n* **15**
beach ball *n* **43**
beak *n* **47**
beans *n* **29**
bear *n* **8**
beard *n* **40**
beautiful *adj* **11**
bed *n* **8**
bedroom *n* **4**
bee *n* **17**
beetle *n* **39**
behind *prep* **12**
belt *n* **51**
bench *n* **21**
between *prep* **28**
bicycle *n* **21**

big *adj* 11
bird *n* 19
birthday party *n* 19
black *adj* 38
black *n* 4
blanket *n* 34
blonde *adj* 38
blue *n* 1
board *n* 1
board game *n* 2
boat *n* 27
body *n* 6
book *n* 5
bookcase *n* 7
bookstore *n* 21
boots *n* 26
bored *adj* 47
borrow *v* 35
bottle *n* 33
bottom *adj* 35
bounce *v* 9
bowl *n* 33
box *n* 52
boy *n* 7
bracelet *n* 48
branch *n* 13
brave *adj* 39
bread *n* 14
break *v* 40
breakfast *n* 12
bridge *n* 34
bring *v* 38
broken *adj* 51
bronze *n* 36
brother *n* 14
brown *adj* 38

brown *n* 4
brush *n* 37
brush my teeth *v* 25
bucket *n* 43
build *v* 44
burger *n* 7
burn *v* 45
bus *n* 24
bus station *n* 24
bus stop *n* 32
butter *n* 44
butterfly *n* 39
button *n* 51
buy *v* 43

C

cabbage *n* 23
cabinet *n* 31
café *n* 21
cake *n* 19
calendar *n* 8
camel *n* 24
camera *n* 34
camp *v* 45
candle *n* 19
candy *n* 16
car *n* 25
card *n* 19
carnival *n* 28
carpet *n* 19
carrot *n* 15
carry *v* 43
cart *n* 33
cartoon *n* 46
castle *n* 27
cat *n* 6, 16

catch *v* 9
catch a bus *v* 13
caterpillar *n* 17
cave *n* 23
ceiling *n* 30
cell phone *n* 31
center *n* 41
cereal *n* 12
chair *n* 16, 19
change *v* 51
charger *n* 31
chat *v* 45
cheap *adj* 50
check *v* 10
cheese *n* 38
chef *n* 32
cherry *n* 20
chess *n* 45
chest *n* 20
chicken *n* 4
chicken *n* 7
child *n* 18
children *n* 10
chin *n* 40
chocolate *n* 44
choose *v* 17
chopsticks *n* 49
circle *n* 17
circle *v* 10
circus *n* 28
city *n* 33
clap *v* 19
class *n* 1
classmate *n* 2
classroom *n* 2
claw *n* 47

clean *adj* **11**

clean *v* **22**

cleaner *n* **50**

climb *v* **15**

clock *n* **16, 42**

close *v* **8**

clothes *n* **7**

cloud *n* **31**

cloudy *adj* **28**

clown *n* **28**

coat *n* **26**

coconut *n* **5**

coffee *n* **36**

cold *adj* **35**

cold *n* **30**

collar *n* **49**

collect *v* **41**

college *n* **33**

color *v* **3**

colors *n* **1**

comb *n* **37**

comet *n* **48**

comic book *n* **46**

compass *n* **48**

competition *n* **50**

complete *v* **29**

computer *n* **28**

concert *n* **52**

cook *v* **16**

cookie *n* **36**

corner *n* **41**

correct *adj* **22**

couch *n* **7**

cough *n* **30**

count *v* **3**

countryside *n* **30**

cousin *n* **14**

cow *n* **4**

crab *n* **46**

crayon *n* **2**

crocodile *n* **24**

cross *v* **10**

crosswalk *n* **32**

crown *n* **51**

cry *v* **26**

cup *n* **33**

curly *adj* **18**

curtains *n* **43**

cushion *n* **19**

cut *v* **41**

cycle *v* **13**

D

dad *n* **3**

dance *v* **11**

dancing *n* **14**

dark *adj* **40**

date *n* **22**

daughter *n* **3**

day *n* **8**

December *n* **p217**

deer *n* **46**

dentist *n* **29**

desert *n* **24**

design *n* **47**

design *v* **49**

designer *n* **48**

desk *n* **16**

diary *n* **43**

dictionary *n* **45**

different *adj* **25**

dining room *n* **4**

dinner *n* **14**

dinosaur *n* **10**

dirty *adj* **11**

do homework *v* **22**

doctor *n* **18**

dog *n* **6, 16**

doll *n* **2**

dolphin *n* **20**

don't like *v* **37**

donkey *n* **19**

door *n* **30**

downstairs *n* **22**

dragonfly *n* **17**

draw *v* **3**

drawing *n* **14**

dream *v* **25**

dress *n* **9**

drink *v* **16**

drinks *n* **17**

drive *v* **13**

driver *n* **24**

drop *v* **50**

drum *n* **52**

dry *adj* **35**

dry *v* **16**

duck *n* **37**

DVD *n* **24**

E

eagle *n* **47**

ear *n* **11**

earache *n* **30**

Earth *n* **34**

east *n* **48**

eat *v* **16**

e-book *n* **21**

egg n 12

eggplant n 23

eight num 2

eighteen num 4

eighty num p216

elbow n 20

elephant n 5

elevator n 12

eleven num 3

email n 21

email v 24

empty adj 46

engine n 52

engineer n 42

English n 44

entrance n 45

envelope n 30

eraser n 5

evening n 8

excited adj 27

exit n 45

expensive adj 50

explore v 49

eye n 11

eyebrow n 40

F

face n 11

factory n 35

fall n 42

fall over v 26

family n 3

far adj 40

farm n 10

farmer n 19

fast adj 44

fat adj 44

father n 3

faucet n 27

favorite adj 25

February n p217

feed v 40

feel v 52

fence n 14

festival n 41

fetch v 40

few adj 46

field n 10

field hockey n 6

fifteen num 3

fifty num p216

find v 29

fingers n 20

finish v 33

fire n 42

fire engine n 25

fire station n 35

firefighter n 18

first adj 50

fish n 29

fish v 18

fishing n 29

fishing rod n 29

five num 1

fix v 44

flag n 43

flashlight n 42

floor n 30

flour n 44

flower n 13

fly n 39

fly v 18

fog n 13

foggy adj 28

food n 32

foot n 23

forest n 27

fork n 49

forty num p216

four num 1

fourteen num 3

fox n 46

Friday n p217

friendly adj 27

friends n 18

fries n 7

frog n 8, 37

front adj 40

fruit n 13

full adj 46

fur n 49

furry adj 44

G

game n 16

garlic n 23

gate n 25

geography n 47

get dressed v 25

get off v 36

get on v 36

giraffe n 5

girl n 7

give v 38, 43

glass n 33

glasses n 37

gloves n 26

glue n 42

glue v 44
goat n 4
goggles n 22
gold n 36
goldfish n 6
golf n 23
gorilla n 26
granddaughter n 9
grandfather n 9
grandmother n 9
grandparents n 9
grandson n 9
grapes n 1
grass n 37
gray adj 38
green n 1
greet v 38
ground n 31
ground floor n 12
group n 18
grow v 41
grown-up n 18
gym n 31
gymnastics n 23

H

hair n 18
hairdresser n 50
half adj 46
half n 41
hall n 22
hand n 20
happy adj 12
hard adj 51
hat n 41
head n 6

headache n 30
headphones n 31
hear v 52
helmet n 15
help v 26
hide v 40
hills n 30
hippo n 5
history n 47
hit v 9
hobbies n 14
hockey stick n 36
hold v 50
home n 14
honey n 44
hop v 32
horse n 4
hospital n 35
hot adj 35
hotel n 41
hour n 42
house n 3
hungry adj 27
hurry v 36
hurt v 26

I

ice n 32
ice cream n 28
ice hockey n 47
ice skates n 36
ice-skating n 47
ill adj 39
in prep 12
in front of prep 12
insects n 31

inside prep 28
instruments n 52
invent v 49
invitation n 16
island n 15

J

jacket n 11
jam n 44
January n p217
jeans n 7
jellyfish n 20
jewelry n 37
jobs n 48
join v 29
journalist n 48
juice n 17
July n p217
jump v 15
June n p217
jungle n 8

K

kangaroo n 26
key n 30
keyboard n 28
kick n 39
kick v 9
king n 51
kitchen n 4
kite n 6
kitten n 16
kiwi n 5
knee n 23
knife n 49

L

ladder n 25
ladybug n 17
lake n 27
lamp n 16
land v 36
languages n 47
laptop n 31
laugh v 45
leaf n 13
learn v 5
left adj 40
leg n 6
lemon n 20
lemonade n 17
lesson n 27
letter n 30
letters n 2
lettuce n 38
library n 31
life jacket n 29
lift v 50
light adj 40
lights n 19
like v 37
lime n 20
lion n 5
lips n 11
listen v 5
little adj 35
living room n 4
lizard n 23
long adj 18
look after v 40
look for v 51
loud adj 40

lounge chair n 41
lunch n 13

M

machine n 42
magazine n 46
mail carrier n 50
make the bed v 25
man n 7
mango n 5
many adj 46
map n 45
March n p217
market n 30
mask n 45
mat n 25
match n 39
match v 10
math n 44
May n p217
meal n 49
meat n 29
meatballs n 14
mechanic n 52
medicine n 45
meet v 34
men n 10
menu n 32
message n 21
metal n 49
microwave n 52
midday n 42
middle adj 35
midnight n 42
milk n 36
milkshake n 17

minute n 42
mirror n 26
mistake n 22
mix v 44
mom n 3
Monday n p217
money n 33
monkey n 8
monster n 10
month n 43
moon n 34
morning n 8
mother n 3
motorcycle n 25
mountain n 27
mouse n 16
mouse n 28
mouth n 40
move v 19
movie n 21
movie star n 21
museum n 33
mushroom n 23
music n 41, 52
musician n 41
mustache n 40

N

name n 30
neck n 6
necklace n 48
nest n 47
net n 29
new adj 25
newspaper n 46
next to prep 12

nice *adj* 9
night *n* 8
nine *num* 2
nineteen *num* 4
ninety *num* **p216**
ninety-eight *num* **p216**
ninety-five *num* **p216**
ninety-four *num* **p216**
ninety-nine *num* **p216**
ninety-one *num* **p216**
ninety-seven *num* **p216**
ninety-six *num* **p216**
ninety-three *num* **p216**
ninety-two *num* **p216**
noisy *adj* 47
noodles *n* 7
north *n* 48
nose *n* 11
notepad *n* 45
November *n* **p217**
numbers *n* 2
nurse *n* 18

O

ocean *n* 15
October *n* **p217**
octopus *n* 20
office *n* 31
old *adj* 9, 25
olives *n* 38
on *prep* 12
one *num* 1
one hundred *num* **p216**
one million *num* **p216**
one thousand *num* **p216**
onion *n* 23

open *v* 8
orange *n* 1
orange *n* 4
order *v* 37
outside *prep* 28
oven *n* 31
over *prep* 28
owl *n* 46

P

paint *n* 2
paint *v* 44
painting *n* 14
pajamas *n* 7
pan *n* 52
pancake *n* 12
panda *n* 26
pants *n* 11
paper *n* 2
parent *n* 18
park *n* 3
parking lot *n* 45
parrot *n* 26
party *n* 16
passenger *n* 24
pasta *n* 14
path *n* 34
pattern *n* 50
paw *n* 49
pay *v* 37
peach *n* 20
pear *n* 5
peas *n* 15
pen *n* 2
pencil *n* 2
penguin *n* 37

people *n* 10
pepper *n* 15
pepper *n* 52
perfume *n* 37
person *n* 10
pets *n* 6
phone *v* 24
photo *n* 34
photographer *n* 48
pick up *v* 8
picnic *n* 34
picture *n* 27
pie *n* 29
pig *n* 19
pilot *n* 38
pineapple *n* 1
pink *n* 4
pizza *n* 7
planet *n* 48
plant *n* 13
plant *v* 41
plastic *n* 49
plate *n* 33
platform *n* 39
play *v* 15, 32
play the guitar *v* 11
play the piano *v* 11
player *n* 39
playground *n* 3
plumber *n* 50
pocket *n* 51
point *v* 5
polar bear *n* 37
police officer *n* 18
polka dots *n* 50
pond *n* 37

pool *n* **41**

pop star *n* **41**

post office *n* **21**

postcard *n* **34**

poster *n* **8**

pot *n* **52**

potato *n* **15**

practice *v* **22**

prepare *v* **37**

present *n* **19**

pretty *adj* **9**

prince *n* **51**

princess *n* **51**

printer *n* **28**

prize *n* **50**

project *n* **27**

pull *v* **50**

puppet *n* **2**

puppy *n* **16**

purple *n* **1**

purse *n* **33, 48**

push *v* **50**

put on *v* **17**

puzzle *n* **27**

puzzle book *n* **46**

pyramid *n* **24**

Q

quarter *n* **41**

queen *n* **51**

question *n* **22**

quiet *adj* **47**

R

rabbit *n* **6**

race *n* **36**

race *v* **33**

radio *n* **24**

railcar *n* **39**

railroad track *n* **39**

rain *n* **13**

rainbow *n* **13**

read *v* **35**

receptionist *n* **50**

rectangle *n* **17**

red *adj* **38**

red *n* **1**

refrigerator *n* **31**

reindeer *n* **37**

relax *v* **22**

remote control *n* **24**

repair *v* **51**

restaurant *n* **32**

rhino *n* **26**

rice *n* **29**

ride *n* **28**

ride a bike *v* **20**

right *adj* **40**

ring *n* **48**

river *n* **23**

road *n* **32**

robot *n* **10**

rock *n* **31**

rocket *n* **34**

rocks *n* **46**

roller skates *n* **15**

roof *n* **14**

rug *n* **7**

ruler *n* **5**

run *v* **13, 15**

S

sad *adj* **12**

sail *v* **18**

salad *n* **38**

salt *n* **52**

same *adj* **25**

sand *n* **15**

sandals *n* **9**

sandcastle *n* **43**

sandwich *n* **13**

Saturday *n* **p217**

sauce *n* **14**

sausage *n* **12**

scared *adj* **27**

scarf *n* **26**

scary *adj* **9**

school *n* **3**

science *n* **44**

scissors *n* **5**

score *n* **39**

score *v* **20**

screen *n* **28**

sea *n* **6**

seagull *n* **6**

seal *n* **37**

search *v* **29, 35**

seasons *n* **42**

seat *n* **21**

seaweed *n* **46**

second *adj* **50**

see *v* **52**

seesaw *n* **21**

sell *v* **43**

send *v* **24**

sentence *n* **22**

September *n* **p217**

suitcase n 38
summer n 42
sun n 34
Sunday n **p217**
sunglasses n 41
sunny adj 28
supermarket n 31
surf v 18
surprised adj 12
swan n 37
sweater n 26
swim v 18
swimming n 22
swimming pool n 22
swimsuit n 22
swing n 21
swing v 32

T

table n 19
table tennis n 23
tablet n 21
tail n 49
take a photo v 11
take off v 36
talk v 24
tall adj 35
taste v 52
taxi n 24
tea n 36
teach v 5
teacher n 1
team n 39
teddy bear n 2
teeth n 29
telephone n 16

telescope n 48
television n 7
tell v 26
ten num 2, **p216**
tennis n 6
tennis racket n 15
tent n 42
theater n 21, 43
thin adj 44
think v 49
third adj 50
thirsty adj 27
thirteen num 3
thirty num **p216**
three num 1
throw v 9
Thursday n **p217**
ticket n 21
tidy adj 47
tidy v 22
tie n 51
tiger n 8
timetable n 44
tire n 52
tired adj 39
toes n 23
toilet n 26
tomato n 38
tongue n 29
toolbox n 42
tools n 42
tooth n 29
toothbrush n 27
toothpaste n 27
top adj 35
tortoise n 23

touch v 19
tour n 34
towel n 22
town n 21
toy box n 8
toy store n 21
toys n 8
tractor n 10
traffic n 32
traffic lights n 32
trailer n 42
train n 39
trash can n 31
travel v 34
tree n 13
triangle n 17
truck n 25
try v 29
T-shirt n 9
Tuesday n **p217**
turn v 32
turn off v 51
turn on v 51
TV n 24
twelve num 3
twenty num 4, **p216**
two num 1

U

uncle n 14
under prep 28
underwear n 7
untidy adj 47
upstairs n 22

V

vacation *n* 38
vegetables *n* 15
vet *n* 18
video *v* 33
video game *n* 10
view *n* 34
village *n* 30
violin *n* 52
visit *v* 38
volleyball *n* 23

W

wait *v* 17
waiter *n* 32
wake up *v* 25
walk *v* 13, 19
wall *n* 25
walrus *n* 37
warm *adj* 35
wash *v* 16
watch *n* 48
watch *v* 33
water *n* 17
water *v* 41
waterfall *n* 23

watermelon *n* 5
wave *n* 15
wave *v* 19
weak *adj* 51
weather *n* 28
website *n* 31
Wednesday *n* **p217**
week *n* 43
weekend *n* 43
weigh *v* 43
west *n* 48
wet *adj* 35
whale *n* 20
wheel *n* 52
whiskers *n* 49
whisper *v* 35
whistle *v* 32
white *n* 4
whole *n* 41
wind *n* 13
window *n* 30
windy *adj* 28
wing *n* 47
winner *n* 36
winter *n* 42
wolf *n* 46

woman *n* 7
women *n* 10
wood *n* 49
woods *n* 30
wool *n* 49
words *n* 1
work *v* 34
write *v* 3

X

X-ray *n* 45

Y

yard *n* 14
year *n* 43
yellow *n* 1
yogurt *n* 13
young *adj* 9

Z

zebra *n* 5
zero *num* **p216**
zipper *n* 51
zoo *n* 33

Common subjects

This is an index of common topics found in the book. Each subject is followed by the weeks it is taught in or the page number it appears on (for example, p216).

Answers

Week 1

1
1. teacher
2. board
3. colors
4. words
5. class

2
1. purple
2. red
3. yellow
4. blue
5. green

3
1. two
2. five
3. four
4. one
5. three

4
1. pineapple
2. grapes
3. apple
4. banana
5. orange

Week 2

1
1. numbers
2. alphabet
3. letters
4. classmate
5. classroom

2
1. doll
2. action figure
3. teddy bear
4. board game
5. puppet

3
1. B
2. A
3. B
4. A
5. A

4
1. eight
2. six
3. nine
4. seven
5. ten

Week 3

1
1. draw
2. color
3. count
4. spell
5. write

2
1. school
2. playground
3. park
4. street
5. house

3
1. eleven
2. thirteen
3. fifteen
4. fourteen
5. twelve

4
1. family
2. father
3. mother
4. son
5. daughter

Week 4

1
1. brown
2. pink
3. orange
4. white
5. black

2
1. B
2. A
3. B
4. A
5. A

3
1. chicken
2. goat
3. sheep
4. cow
5. horse

4
1. seventeen
2. twenty
3. eighteen
4. sixteen
5. nineteen

Week 5

1
1. zebra
2. hippo
3. lion
4. giraffe
5. elephant

2
1. scissors
2. book
3. ruler
4. eraser
5. backpack

3
1. listen
2. teach
3. learn
4. point
5. answer

4
1. kiwi
2. pear
3. watermelon
4. coconut
5. mango

Week 6

1
1. B
2. A
3. B
4. A
5. B

2
1. head
2. leg
3. body
4. arm
5. neck

3
1. field hockey
2. tennis
3. baseball
4. basketball
5. badminton

4
1. sea
2. seagull
3. kite
4. ship
5. ball

Week 7

1
1. girl
2. man
3. boy
4. baby
5. woman

2
1. B
2. A
3. A
4. B
5. A

3
1. couch
2. rug
3. armchair
4. bookcase
5. television

4
1. pizza
2. noodles
3. burger
4. fries
5. chicken

Week 8

1
1. tiger
2. frog
3. monkey
4. jungle
5. bear

2
1. A
2. B
3. A
4. A
5. B

3
1. sit down
2. open
3. close
4. pick up
5. stand up

4
1. afternoon
2. night
3. morning
4. evening
5. day

Week 9

1
1. grandparents
2. grandmother
3. grandfather
4. grandson
5. granddaughter

2
1. T-shirt
2. dress
3. sandals
4. shoes
5. shorts

3
1. pretty
2. old
3. scary
4. young
5. nice

4
1. catch
2. hit
3. kick
4. throw
5. bounce

Week 10

1
1. person
2. women
3. children
4. people
5. men

2
1. B
2. A
3. B
4. A
5. A

3
1. tractor
2. field
3. farm
4. animals
5. barn

4
1. dinosaur
2. skateboard
3. video game
4. robot
5. monster

Week 11

1
1. eye
2. lips
3. nose
4. ear
5. face

2
1. A
2. B
3. A
4. A
5. B

3
1. beautiful
2. clean
3. small
4. dirty
5. big

4
1. shirt
2. baseball cap
3. skirt
4. pants
5. jacket

Week 12

1
1. in
2. in front of
3. behind
4. next to
5. on

2
1. cereal
2. breakfast
3. egg
4. pancake
5. sausage

3
1. balcony
2. elevator
3. apartment building
4. ground floor
5. apartment

4
1. surprised
2. sad
3. afraid
4. happy
5. angry

Week 13

1
1. A
2. A
3. B
4. A
5. B

2
1. leaf
2. branch
3. tree
4. plant
5. flower

3
1. storm
2. wind
3. fog
4. rain
5. rainbow

4
1. snack
2. yogurt
3. fruit
4. sandwich
5. lunch

Week 14

1
1. roof
2. fence
3. yard
4. shed
5. home

2
1. drawing
2. dancing
3. painting
4. sports
5. hobbies

3
1. uncle
2. aunt
3. cousin
4. brother
5. sister

4
1. pasta
2. sauce
3. dinner
4. bread
5. meatballs

Week 15

1
1. carrot
2. peas
3. vegetables
4. potato
5. pepper

2
1. ocean
2. wave
3. beach
4. sand
5. island

3
1. helmet
2. sneakers
3. bat
4. tennis racket
5. roller skates

4
1. run
2. skip
3. play
4. climb
5. jump

Week 16

1
1. candy
2. party
3. game
4. invitation
5. balloon

2
1. cook
2. eat
3. wash
4. dry
5. drink

3
1. cat
2. mouse
3. dog
4. puppy
5. kitten

4
1. lamp
2. clock
3. telephone
4. desk
5. chair

Week 17

1
1. ask
2. choose
3. wait
4. put on
5. shop

2
1. ladybug
2. bee
3. ant
4. dragonfly
5. caterpillar

3
1. juice
2. drinks
3. water
4. lemonade
5. milkshake

4
1. triangle
2. circle
3. rectangle
4. square
5. shapes

Week 18

1
1. A
2. B
3. B
4. A
5. B

2
1. hair
2. short
3. straight
4. long
5. curly

3
1. surf
2. fish
3. fly
4. swim
5. sail

4
1. child
2. grown-up
3. parent
4. group
5. friends

Week 19

1
1. move
2. walk
3. touch
4. clap
5. wave

2
1. bird
2. donkey
3. stable
4. pig
5. farmer

3
1. present
2. card
3. birthday party
4. candle
5. cake

4
1. carpet
2. cushion
3. lights
4. chair
5. table

Week 20

1
1. A
2. B
3. A
4. B
5. A

2
1. dolphin
2. jellyfish
3. octopus
4. shark
5. whale

3
1. fingers
2. shoulder
3. elbow
4. hand
5. chest

4
1. lemon
2. cherry
3. strawberry
4. peach
5. lime

Week 21

1
1. tablet
2. e-book
3. message
4. apps
5. email

2
1. bookstore
2. post office
3. toy store
4. café
5. town

3
1. seat
2. theater
3. movie star
4. ticket
5. movie

4
1. A
2. B
3. A
4. A
5. B

Week 22

1
1. hall
2. upstairs
3. downstairs
4. stairs
5. basement

2
1. do homework
2. tidy
3. practice
4. relax
5. clean

3
1. towel
2. swimming pool
3. swimsuit
4. goggles
5. swimming

4
1. correct
2. question
3. date
4. mistake
5. sentence

Week 23

1
1. onion
2. garlic
3. cabbage
4. mushroom
5. eggplant

2
1. river
2. waterfall
3. cave
4. lizard
5. tortoise

3
1. golf
2. volleyball
3. gymnastics
4. table tennis
5. soccer

4
1. back
2. stomach
3. knee
4. foot
5. toes

Week 24

1
1. A
2. B
3. B
4. A
5. B

2
1. camel
2. pyramid
3. desert
4. snake
5. crocodile

3
1. taxi
2. passenger
3. bus
4. driver
5. bus station

4
1. phone
2. email
3. send
4. shout
5. talk

Week 25

1
1. step
2. mat
3. wall
4. ladder
5. gate

2
1. car
2. truck
3. motorcycle
4. fire engine
5. ambulance

3
1. B
2. A
3. A
4. B
5. A

4
1. same
2. different
3. new
4. favorite
5. old

Week 26

1
1. tell
2. cry
3. help
4. hurt
5. fall over

2
1. kangaroo
2. gorilla
3. rhino
4. panda
5. parrot

3
1. boots
2. sweater
3. scarf
4. coat
5. gloves

4
1. bathtub
2. toilet
3. mirror
4. shelf
5. shower

Week 27

1
1. scared
2. excited
3. friendly
4. thirsty
5. hungry

2
1. soap
2. sink
3. toothpaste
4. toothbrush
5. faucet

3
1. project
2. puzzle
3. picture
4. story
5. lesson

4
1. forest
2. mountain
3. castle
4. lake
5. boat

Week 28

1
1. A
2. B
3. B
4. A
5. B

2
1. foggy
2. sunny
3. weather
4. windy
5. cloudy

3
1. mouse
2. printer
3. computer
4. screen
5. keyboard

4
1. circus
2. ride
3. ice cream
4. carnival
5. clown

Week 29

1
1. search
2. find
3. join
4. complete
5. try

2
1. fish
2. fishing
3. fishing rod
4. net
5. life jacket

3
1. teeth
2. tongue
3. tooth
4. smile
5. dentist

4
1. beans
2. meat
3. rice
4. soup
5. pie

Week 30

1
1. village
2. hills
3. countryside
4. woods
5. market

2
1. letter
2. address
3. envelope
4. stamp
5. name

3
1. B
2. A
3. B
4. A
5. B

4
1. ceiling
2. window
3. door
4. floor
5. key

Week 31

1
1. B
2. B
3. B
4. A
5. A

2
1. office
2. library
3. stadium
4. gym
5. supermarket

3
1. stove
2. trash can
3. oven
4. cabinet
5. refrigerator

4
1. rock
2. sky
3. cloud
4. ground
5. insects

Week 32

1
1. B
2. A
3. A
4. A
5. B

2
1. menu
2. restaurant
3. chef
4. food
5. waiter

3
1. play
2. hop
3. turn
4. swing
5. whistle

4
1. road
2. bus stop
3. traffic
4. crosswalk
5. traffic lights

Week 33

1
1. plate
2. bottle
3. glass
4. bowl
5. cup

2
1. A
2. B
3. A
4. A
5. B

3
1. purse
2. shopping
3. basket
4. money
5. cart

4
1. zoo
2. city
3. museum
4. college
5. skyscraper

Week 34

1
1. travel
2. work
3. speak
4. meet
5. show

2
1. astronaut
2. Earth
3. sun
4. moon
5. rocket

3
1. bridge
2. stream
3. path
4. picnic
5. blanket

4
1. photo
2. view
3. camera
4. tour
5. postcard

Week 35

1
1. B
2. A
3. A
4. A
5. B

2
1. little
2. bottom
3. middle
4. tall
5. top

3
1. warm
2. dry
3. wet
4. cold
5. hot

4
1. study
2. whisper
3. search
4. read
5. borrow

Week 36

1
1. tea
2. cookie
3. coffee
4. milk
5. sugar

2
1. gold
2. winner
3. silver
4. bronze
5. race

3
1. take off
2. land
3. hurry
4. get off
5. get on

4
1. B
2. A
3. A
4. B
5. A

Week 37

1
1. like
2. don't like
3. pay
4. order
5. prepare

2
1. comb
2. glasses
3. brush
4. perfume
5. jewelry

3
1. penguin
2. polar bear
3. seal
4. reindeer
5. walrus

4
1. grass
2. frog
3. pond
4. swan
5. duck

Week 38

1
1. pilot
2. airport
3. vacation
4. suitcase
5. airplane

2
1. bring
2. arrive
3. visit
4. give
5. greet

3
1. brown
2. blonde
3. red
4. black
5. gray

4
1. salad
2. lettuce
3. tomato
4. cheese
5. olives

Week 39

1
1. match
2. kick
3. team
4. score
5. player

2
1. beetle
2. fly
3. butterfly
4. snail
5. spider

3
1. brave
2. sick
3. sore
4. tired
5. ill

4
1. B
2. A
3. B
4. B
5. A

Week 40

1
1. light
2. awake
3. dark
4. asleep
5. loud

2
1. hide
2. fetch
3. feed
4. break
5. look after

3
1. far
2. left
3. back
4. right
5. front

4
1. mouth
2. chin
3. eyebrow
4. mustache
5. beard

Week 41

1
1. whole
2. corner
3. half
4. center
5. quarter

2
1. pool
2. hat
3. hotel
4. lounge chair
5. sunglasses

3
1. B
2. A
3. B
4. A
5. A

4
1. collect
2. plant
3. water
4. grow
5. cut

Week 42

1
1. clock
2. midday
3. minute
4. midnight
5. hour

2
1. fire
2. trailer
3. tent
4. flashlight
5. smoke

3
1. summer
2. winter
3. fall
4. spring
5. seasons

4
1. glue
2. engineer
3. toolbox
4. tools
5. machine

Week 43

1
1. weigh
2. buy
3. give
4. sell
5. carry

2
1. actor
2. curtains
3. stage
4. singer
5. theater

3
1. flag
2. beach ball
3. bucket
4. shovel
5. sandcastle

4
1. month
2. week
3. year
4. diary
5. weekend

Week 44

1
1. art
2. math
3. science
4. English
5. timetable

2
1. build
2. paint
3. mix
4. fix
5. glue

3
1. butter
2. jam
3. chocolate
4. flour
5. honey

4
1. furry
2. slow
3. fat
4. fast
5. thin

Week 45

1
1. exit
2. parking lot
3. stores
4. entrance
5. shopping center

2
1. student
2. map
3. chess
4. dictionary
5. notepad

3
1. medicine
2. X-ray
3. bandage
4. band-aid
5. mask

4
1. burn
2. laugh
3. chat
4. camp
5. sleep

Week 46

1
1. wolf
2. owl
3. deer
4. squirrel
5. fox

2
1. crab
2. shell
3. rocks
4. seaweed
5. starfish

3
1. full
2. empty
3. half
4. few
5. many

4
1. A
2. B
3. B
4. B
5. A

Week 47

1
1. geography
2. design
3. history
4. languages
5. subjects

2
1. nest
2. beak
3. wing
4. claw
5. eagle

3
1. noisy
2. quiet
3. untidy
4. tidy
5. bored

4
1. A
2. B
3. A
4. B
5. B

Week 48

1
1. compass
2. north
3. west
4. east
5. south

2
1. jobs
2. designer
3. journalist
4. artist
5. photographer

3
1. ring
2. bracelet
3. purse
4. necklace
5. watch

4
1. comet
2. space
3. planet
4. stars
5. telescope

Week 49

1
1. B
2. A
3. B
4. A
5. B

2
1. metal
2. stone
3. wood
4. plastic
5. wool

3
1. whiskers
2. paw
3. tail
4. collar
5. fur

4
1. invent
2. think
3. explore
4. act
5. design

Week 50

1
1. pull
2. hold
3. push
4. drop
5. lift

2
1. stripes
2. expensive
3. polka dots
4. pattern
5. cheap

3
1. first
2. competition
3. prize
4. second
5. third

4
1. cleaner
2. receptionist
3. hairdresser
4. plumber
5. mail carrier

Week 51

1
1. change
2. look for
3. turn on
4. turn off
5. repair

2
1. tie
2. button
3. zipper
4. pocket
5. belt

3
1. strong
2. soft
3. hard
4. broken
5. weak

4
1. princess
2. king
3. prince
4. crown
5. queen

Week 52

1
1. pepper
2. salt
3. microwave
4. pot
5. pan

2
1. drum
2. music
3. concert
4. instruments
5. violin

3
1. taste
2. smell
3. see
4. hear
5. feel

4
1. B
2. A
3. B
4. A
5. B

Acknowledgments

The publisher would like to thank:

Adam Brackenbury for design and illustration assistance; Edwood Burn for illustration assistance; Ankita Awasthi Tröger for proofreading; Abigail Ellis for indexing; Jennette ElNaggar for Americanization; and Rakesh Kumar, Priyanka Sharma, and Saloni Singh for jacket design assistance.